THE NINE BATONS

An inspiring account of mindset change, grit and achievement by NCC cadets.

Col M P Dinesh

INDIA • SINGAPORE • MALAYSIA

Copyright © Colonel M P Dinesh 2024
All Rights Reserved.

ISBN 978-9-33411-412-6

This book has been published with all efforts taken to make the material error-free after the consent of the author. However, the author and the publisher do not assume and hereby disclaim any liability to any party for any loss, damage, or disruption caused by errors or omissions, whether such errors or omissions result from negligence, accident, or any other cause.

While every effort has been made to avoid any mistake or omission, this publication is being sold on the condition and understanding that neither the author nor the publishers or printers would be liable in any manner to any person by reason of any mistake or omission in this publication or for any action taken or omitted to be taken or advice rendered or accepted on the basis of this work. For any defect in printing or binding the publishers will be liable only to replace the defective copy by another copy of this work then available.

*A fictional account inspired by real-life incidences,
laced with imagination to create a better impact and
bring out strongly the time-tested life lessons for
mindset change and success*

To my wife Suja

*An epitome of perseverance and unconditional love which
are so much related to each other.*

Contents

Introduction

Happiness is the Discovery of Self

*"Because creation is finished, what you desire already exists.
It is excluded from your view because you see only the
content of your consciousness"*

– Neville Goddard

We are born with limitless possibilities, but as we grow up, we start drawing boundaries around us on what and how much we can do. At times it is based on the outcome of our limited experiences involving setbacks and failure. Mostly it is based on other's experiences and opinions about us, themselves and the world. These boundaries often become the framework of our perception. That perception dictates the way we view and approach life situations. Perceptions are dangerous when we let them grow unconsciously, but are facilitators when it has been crafted through their conscious cultivation with complete awareness. Over time we allow these perceptions to crystallize by repeating them to ourselves, often inadvertently while facing what life throws at us till we see them as long-lasting unchangeable "truths" about ourselves. When a person is not happy with his circumstances and tries to change them, he makes the effort to change and craft a new self from the existing framework of perceptions and therefore finds every attempt failing, reinforcing the biased concept within oneself about oneself. External circumstances are merely a reflection of the framework that one carries within himself.

But unlike a seed that's fallen on a barren desert and is condemned to whither and perish unless favoured by a chanced blizzard to take it to a more favourable ground, man need not submit to the diktats of destiny and nor does he need to remain stuck in the episodes of the past. He has a mind and soul always yearning to fulfil the potential bestowed upon him. His mind has the innate ability to look for possibilities. When he takes time to listen to the groans of the unfulfilled soul, he sparks a desire within himself. And when he chooses to focus on victories rather than defeats, blessings rather than deprivations, joyful moments rather than painful memories, he develops a sense of faith. And as *Napolean Hill* said, "desire backed by faith, knows no such word as impossible". This combination of desire and faith sets within a person the vibration that attracts people and circumstances that have resonating wavelengths.

As a serendipitous occurrence, they find themselves in situations and in the company of people which proves to be life-changing. One thing leads to another. Chance encounters lead to inspiration which leads to a changed approach which in turn brings new results and finally gives a person a completely changed outlook towards oneself and the world.

A man therefore at all times is presented with a choice. The choice is to be either governed by the setting in his system manufactured by past events and experiences or to listen to voices from within shouting for the fulfilment of purpose. And the conflict between the two has to be endured by the man in every moment of his life. The victor in this battle is decided by what the man chooses to do. Live life with complete awareness and embark on a journey towards unseen and unlimited opportunities and possibilities or let the unconscious tendencies manufactured by past experiences and opinions take life through the path of least resistance leading to the destination of least fulfilment. But unlike what may be perceived this conscious effort to live a life of complete awareness is not dreary, monotonous and draining, instead, it's enriching, rejuvenating and rewarding in terms of joy and happiness occurring as a consequence of enhanced self-esteem and the feeling of the life being under one's control.

Though this book is a fictional narrative of the journey of young cadets of the National Cadet Corps, it is inspired by real-life incidents. The book brings out the pains and struggles of the cadets, each one of whom is fighting the demons of their past and trying to move forward against the drag of the shackles of the past. The book also brings out the vulnerabilities of the mentors and brings forth their insecurities while they put a brave front before the cadets. The book tries to highlight the true reward that the National Cadet Corps as an organisation provides to the cadet. That reward is the opportunity to break the shackles of the past and traverse a fresh trajectory of self-discovery. It is written with the intention of not only helping the cadets to realise their potential but will also be found relevant and useful for anyone who is looking for ways to realise the full potential that he/ she was born with. To realise the potential to the fullest is the responsibility of every human being because unless it is achieved, real happiness will continue to evade.

Colonel M P Dinesh

08 Apr 2024

Chapter 1

The Doubtful Beginning

---◆◆---

"Not a very bright lot, can't hope for as many medals as we got last year", said the Training Colonel with a glum expression on his face, as he scanned the group of cadets in front of him. These cadets were appearing for the written exam for the "Best Cadet" event which was part of the competitions held between various groups of the NCC Directorate as part of the preparations for the prestigious Republic Day Camp or RDC held at the national level at New Delhi. NCC is organised into 17 Directorates with each Directorate having about 5 to 6 groups and each group with about 10 battalions or what is loosely termed as units. Each unit looks after a cluster of about 20+ institutions which includes both schools and colleges. "Last year we had such talent that it was difficult to decide on the winner and whom to nominate to represent the directorate at the Republic Day Camp at New Delhi", the Training Colonel continued. Lieutenant Colonel Ajit Menon could fathom the disappointment that the Training Colonel was experiencing and it only added to his nervousness. This was his second encounter with the Training Colonel, the first one was during the selection and preparation for *Thal Sainik Camp*. The experience then had not been too pleasant due to the Training Colonel's proclivity for sarcasm and patronising attitude. Menon was in charge of training the cadets for the "Best cadets" category and the cadets trained by him had excelled at the national level. This outcome made him a favourite for training the "Best Cadets" in future events too, and he had become conscious of this image of his. His expectations from others and himself were the reason why the rants of the Training colonel were making him anxious.

Menon had been detailed by none other than Commodore Ganguly, the top man at the Directorate, to select and train the Directorate team for the RDC, especially the cadets who were to participate in the best cadet event at the national level. NCC, the uniformed youth organisation of India, the largest such organisation in the world, is made up of volunteer students from schools and colleges. It is staffed with service personnel from the armed forces to train the cadets in basic military drills and knowledge. The organisation has a stated overall objective of grooming well-disciplined future citizens for the country. Ironically, to achieve this grand objective, the staff from the three wings of the defence forces posted to this organisation are those who have exhausted all avenues for progression in their armed forces career. So, a mention of NCC in officer's club gatherings if not greeted with a condescending glance will be discarded with a cold indifference. The topics immediately gets switched over to the appointments being tenanted in the more happening branches and departments of the Indian Army. Therefore, an officer posted in the NCC has to delve deep into his last reserves of intrinsic motivation and needs to skip most of the steps of Pavlov's ladder and force himself to perch on the step of self-actualisation to fulfil the huge responsibility of nurturing young minds to become citizens who can contribute effectively to the nation. With no badges to flaunt, he has to nudge hard those regions of his brain responsible for altruism to find a sense of purpose for serving in the organisation. If one can achieve that, then one finds himself in the state of flow wherein one works only for the compensation in terms of fulfilment and the blissful contentment that accompanies the state of flow that the mind finds itself in.

Menon knew the pitfalls of intrinsic motivation. External motivators though transient, are easy but intrinsic motivation is a struggle. It is an everyday struggle between the two selves. One screams for the status quo and the other urging to go out of the comfort zone. The struggle is especially difficult in NCC because moving out of the comfort zone has no tangible benefits, only intangibles like job satisfaction, happiness of altruism etc. The human mind which is habituated to receiving materialistic rewards finds it quite hard to accept the intangible rewards even though these rewards give long-term satisfaction to any person. A paradigm shift in perception is not just difficult but uncomfortable too. A slight slip, and the self-doubt starts creeping in and it is back to the bottom and one has to start all over again, all alone, by himself. There was another reason for his nervousness as he heard the despondent words of the Training Colonel. He was aware of how negative manifestations can lead to negative outcomes and that a deliberate attempt is required to be made to come out of the abyss of involuntary thinking about negative experiences and possible outcomes. His life was an example of how a slide into negativity could take one down the spiral of failures and desperation. As a school student, he had always stood first in his class, he was good in academics and was the favourite of many a teacher. He had represented his school and college in debates at the national level and was elected as college president and then as the university union councillor. And when he entered the gates of IMA, he was looking forward to being among the best once again. But the morning run on the first day in the academy changed it all. He was used to being the first always and the same instincts told him to take action to repeat the experiences without the inkling that the context had changed. There is an undesirable part of being habituated, even for excellence, and that is the drawback of creating a habit towards aiming for favourable outcomes rather than focusing on the more beneficial habit of positive processes. Making a habit of standing first is an example of the former while creating a habit of working hard on anything to become as perfect as possible in a skill or ability, irrespective of the outcome, is an example of the latter. Menon was soon going to discover the pitfalls of simply focusing on the outcome. Menon's self-image, on that fateful morning, was going to receive the rude shock of facing failure, of going through the feeling of being among the last few, the straggler and the tail-ender, of being ridiculed for not being enough. As the run progressed, he could feel his lungs gasping for oxygen, his body screaming at being taken out of the comfort zone of academic pursuits and pushed into the unfamiliar field of physical exertion. His legs started giving way, he started slowing down and one after other the cadets started overtaking him. For the first time, he experienced the ugly feeling of being left behind, of not being at the top

As if this humiliation wasn't enough, the senior cadets heaped on him the choicest of profanities for his lack of physical abilities. For a person who never heard such cuss words in his life, who was always on the podium to receive accolades, the experience wasn't just humiliating, it was frightening. He started sweating less because of the physical strain but more because of the horror of seeing his self, crumbling right in front of his eyes.

As the sweat started flowing down his sideburns he looked up to see the Training Colonel staring at him with a smirk on his face. The human brain can't differentiate between the real and the imaginary. Even after so many years, he could remember that dreadful morning in its vivid details. The sweat moving down his sideburns had brought him back to the present and was glad to come out of the experience that he was reliving. Menon staggered up from his chair and walked up to the young lad who was bent over his desk attempting the questions on the paper in front of him. "What's your name?, How do you find the question paper?", he asked. "Sir Aashish Ahlawat", it's a bit tough sir". Menon had a good look at the beaming face that also carried a slight hint of embarrassment possibly because he found the paper beyond his level of knowledge and ability. But something about that cadet gave him an intuition regarding the cadet's capability. Menon, having been part of the assessment system, called it the assessor's intuition. "That cadet seems to have potential", Menon said as he came back and sat on the chair. "Naah", the Training Colonel dismissed the comment along with a wave of his hand and then started ranting about how he had very meticulously carried out the selection in the previous year and how the entire credit for the good performance must go only to him. The doubts and uncertainty that Menon had tried to remove by looking for some hope in the young cadet came back with renewed vengeance. He had to find a way to shake off the negative thoughts and the fear of failure, which had started gripping him even before he commenced the training of cadets. He stood up and went to the rear of the examination hall. He wanted to carry out some quiet contemplation. He had great faith and belief in the power of thoughts, he was convinced beyond doubt that the reality is created by what goes inside the head of a person. He knew the ultimate truth, which was so convincingly propounded by Earl Nightingale whom he considered as his mentor, that one becomes what one thinks most of the time. Something which everyone has experienced in their lives but only a few choose to accept and carry it as their philosophy. And it perturbed him to realise that what he was thinking now wasn't a harbinger of anything even remotely purposeful or constructive. He needed to rewire to change the thoughts coming to his mind.

As he sat down and looked ahead to the rows of cadets, busy in attempting the questions, he searched for

Rashi, Mahesh and Tarun among the cadets who were sitting in neat lines attempting their exam. These three Cadets had provided validation to his philosophy and his idea of self-development. These were the Cadets about whom, everyone thought had no chance of making it big, but had proved everyone wrong. He wanted a glimpse of these cadets to get his belief back. He wanted to see them so that it would help him to put the negativity behind him and spark some hope in himself. As he stared up the hall, he soon drifted to the days of training camps leading to the "Thal Sainik Camp", a camp held at the national capital exclusively for the army cadets. The naval and air wings have their equivalent camps called "Nau Sainik Camp" and "Vayu Sainik Camp" respectively. The training for that camp too had started on a similar note, as what he was listening to now, with voices of discouragement and pessimism filling his environment on most of the days. He recollected how some of the officers had provided him advice, at times out of sympathy and at times with a patronising attitude, that he was wasting time and resources hoping for a very unlikely result. He was told that the Cadets that he was trying to train were no match for the Cadets from MCC, Loyola and Presidency, the finest colleges of Chennai. But finally, his Cadets from the Government colleges of Tenkasi and Marthandam prevailed not just over the high-profile colleges of Chennai but went on to win the Best Cadet event at New Delhi. As a smile started forming on his face he could feel his confidence too building within him. He closed his eyes to visualise the training that he would commence once the selection process was over. He imagined the morning routine, the run with the cadets, the classes that he would take, and the vibrancy of the responses from the cadets. He could hear the motivational talk that he would be giving to the cadets, the focused attention and the determined look on their faces. He could feel the goosebumps rising. The Training Colonel was busy on his mobile with his usual rant about the lack of quality of Cadets this year, but Menon was far away in the training ground with his cadets. The cadets for whom he was visualising the training had no faces or no names yet, but Menon knew that it didn't matter. He was clear about the path that he had to take to mould the raw material to the substance of steel. And it suddenly dawned upon him that it is the clarity about your goals that creates motivation and that motivation was simply a by-product of the clarity that one has about the set objectives. His visualisation of the training that he would commence soon for the selected cadets filled him up with energy and enthusiasm. The negativity around him didn't matter anymore. The images that he was visualising had made him immune to it since he was focused now on his purpose alone and not on anything else. He stood up and took another stroll around the examination hall and he found that every cadet seemed fit enough to become the best cadet. That indeed was the truth. Anyone can become whatever he/she wished to and the only factor that stood in between a person and his goals was the person himself. The scene was the same but his changed perception had changed the scenario for Menon. He could now spot Mahesh, Rashi and Arun in the hall. Every cadet showed some resemblance to his three cadets from the TSC training days. The joyfulness that he was experiencing must have been reflecting on his face for he found a Junior Wing cadet looking at him as if wondering about the reason for his sudden joy. He nodded and smiled at her who resumed with her writing after the brief distraction. Shreya, that junior wing cadet didn't realise at that moment how her life was going to change for her forever.

"Believe me, this time our Directorate will perform poorly in the competitions.", the words fell on Menon's ears as he walked closer to the dais where the Training Colonel was sitting. "Last year it was because of my flawless selection that our Cadets did so well. The potential of the cadets and the selection by me was the deciding factor for the outstanding results, it wasn't due to any efforts of the trainers". Menon wondered if the Training Colonel was reading his mind and was becoming aware of the plan that was getting formulated in his mind. Menon knew that he needed to shut down this negativity. He picked up the plastic chair and started walking towards the rear of the examination hall. "Sir, I will keep a check from the rear," he said as he walked away from the Colonel once again. He wanted to keep himself away from his not-so-encouraging presence and vibes. There are three ways to address a problem. The first one is to try to change the situation to your liking and comfort. The second is to change the perception towards the situation and when nothing helps, accept the situation and ignore it or walk away from it. Menon chose the third option after having tried the other two.

From the rear of the examination hall, he looked up at the rows of cadets, many of whom were either doing nothing or were trying to look to their sides hoping to get a glimpse of others' papers. However, the distances between the cadets were too large for their efforts to be successful. The question paper that was set by the Training Colonel was quite tough and there was less likelihood of such an assessment being able to carry out significant discrimination of the capabilities of cadets. Menon had always held the view that there needs to be a difference between assessment for selection and assessment of performance post-training. If assessment standards are set too high at the selection stage, beyond the level of an average cadet and not taking into consideration realistic training standards, then every cadet underperforms and the selectors don't get sufficient data on the potential of a cadet. Assessment for selection should be aimed at identifying qualities in a cadet that are critical for absorbing the nuances of training and not just for testing the present level of knowledge. This is different from periodic assessments carried out during the training that are done to observe the assimilation of the training syllabus by the trainees. The Training Colonel, by setting a difficult question paper seemed to be crafting a pessimistic scenario and then proving that his predictions were correct. Just when Menon started to wonder about what the agenda of Training Colonel could be, he realised with a start, that he was getting sucked into the cycle of negative thoughts and perception. He needed something to get out of it. He needed to feed himself with thoughts that could change his disposition. He forced his awareness to the fact that it was his disposition, not someone else's, and it was his thoughts that were creating the disposition and therefore it was his choice. And he firmly believed that "THERE ALWAYS IS A CHOICE". He decided to choose what thoughts he must let in and what he must filter out. And what else could be more encouraging than the thoughts of Rashi, Mahesh and Tarun?

THE REVERIE

Chapter 2

Unfolding of the Assignment

Menon was aware of the dangers of clinging on to the past, both good and bad. He knew and was convinced that one can never aspire to move forward if one is busy looking backwards and that the best part of your life should never be in the past but something for which you work in the present and look forward to in the future. While he did hold these philosophies close to his heart, yet being an open-minded and well-read man, he was also conscious of the fact that there are blurring of the lines between what seemed like contradicting philosophies. Therefore, while he did believe in looking ahead, he knew that the past has a lot of lessons to offer, from which to learn and also transform a person's mood of despair and despondency to a more agreeable one. Menon needed the latter use of the past now, to dispel the prevailing air of pessimism about the cadets who were busy writing the exam without any inkling of how they were being perceived.

Menon leaned back slightly on the chair and while he was conscious of his task as the invigilator, he decided to take his mind back to the days at Idiyapatti, the NCC Training Academy in the spiritually and culturally rich town of Madurai. The very thought of Idiyappatti brought a faint smile to Menon's face. The wilderness was filled with Acacia trees, the narrow long and lonely roads on which one met only an odd villager from the nearby village which had only a handful of mud houses. The uneven landscape was scattered with black palms, and the early morning sunrays played peek-a-boo with the palm leaves. The only other sound that broke the chain of thoughts of a person immersed in himself while walking on narrow roads here was the loud and cheerful "Jai Hind" by the cadets who were out for their morning PT with their "*Ustaads*". The long walks in the morning in fact were quite helpful in crafting the plan for the day and the serene ambience stimulated innovative and practical ideas that could be used for training. These walks were also the occasion when Menon had sowed the seeds of "NINE BATONS". It was to these narrow-deserted roads, that Menon had first disclosed his desire of winning the Nine Batons. The roads had given him silent company and went along with him as he murmured his dream, which would have been considered audacious by any standards of the wildest imagination. The idea to win all the Nine Batons at the Republic Day Camp by a single directorate was not just fantastic but would have only invited ridicule from anyone with whom he would have shared. Menon therefore had decided to share it with the winding roads of Idiyappati and thus to the Universe. He knew that the answer from the universe to deep desires is always a vehement "YES".

As the memories of the past sashayed across his mind, he could observe the changing state of his mind. A soothing pleasantness started enveloping his entire body and mind. The same examination hall, which was filled with gloom, was now looking bright and hopeful. He took a glance across the classroom, a conscious activity towards his duty as an invigilator and then finding the cadets engrossed in their activity, slid back into the inspiring environs of "*Idiyapatti*". He took some time to once more appreciate the enormity of the power of one's mind to change the external reality. He could feel the strength of an invisible force flowing through his veins as he realised that a man has absolute control over his thoughts, mood and emotions. He acknowledged that external circumstances, other's opinions and actions have little impact on you and you always have a choice to either let it affect you or to deflect it as per your sole wish. This realisation was creating an unexplainable vibration inside him. It was as if all the cells were in harmonic resonance. The realisation that he could craft his circumstances as per his wish, gave him a feeling of freedom that he had started experiencing quite frequently in the past few years. The realisation that one need not follow any template of the past or the so-called time-tested practices, made him more open-minded and discriminative while listening to routine conversations.

As he settled comfortably into the beautiful reverie he recollected that it was in May 2019, while driving down from Chennai to his unit at Tirunelveli, a sleepy town in southern Tamilnadu, that Menon had got a call from his superior officer asking him to take up the task of training the cadets of the NCC Group for the "Best Cadet" event that was to be held during the "All India Thal Sainik Camp". His credentials of being a qualified assessor and trainer must have prompted the senior officer to task him for this job. Menon was asked to divert from his intended destination which was his unit and told to report to NCC Training Area at Idiyappati. With some difficulty, Menon was able to find the location. After a series of stone queries and Acacia forests, NTA jumped out in his view. The majestic compound of NTA was a stark contrast to the surrounding environment. The huge freshly painted office complex with a row of trees in front of it, the auditorium and dining hall complex and the cadet's barracks looked as if they had appeared out of some magician's wave of hand in the otherwise vast expanse of abandoned stone queries and thorny forests interspersed with a few dilapidated small huts of the sparsely populated village of Idiayyapatti. Menon chuckled at the irony that the majestic NTA was commonly and usually referred to by the name of its humble companion, the *Idiyappati village*. This village like any other in Tamilnadu bore the symptoms of a water deficit area like the thorny vegetation, dry earth and air and hardly any water bodies of significance. Tamilnadu, the southern state of the country was deprived of the monsoons by the western ghats which forced the rain-bearing clouds to shed all its precious load on the western state of Kerala. The state was reeling under the intense heat of summer. Despite being from Kerala, Menon sympathised with this state he was currently in which was always in a state of conflict with other states over water. Nature had been unfair to this state. On one side of the Ghats, in Kerala, were lush green forests filled with myriad forms of vegetation and on this side, the only trees that showed the grit to sustain were the small leafed thorny short-height Acacias.

Menon looked for a parking space to park his car and he stepped out of the cool interiors of his air-conditioned car into the blazing heat outside. The stark temperature difference immediately had the effect and Menon could feel the sweat beads rolling down the sides of his cheeks and the temple. By the time he reached the entrance to the auditorium, where he presumed the cadets and officials would be, he was sweating profusely. As he took his clean white handkerchief to wipe the sweat, a smart young lad in Khakis approached him " May I get some water for you, sir?" The boy cadet was tall, athletic and with a chiselled jawline. He wore a neatly ironed uniform and spoke with an air of friendly confidence. Menon during the conversation got to know that the name of the cadet was Mahesh and was from a local NCC unit at Madurai and was the ward of an ex-serviceman. Little did the two know that this chance encounter was going to have a significant impact on their lives. After responding to the smart salute by the young cadet and thanking him for the glass of water that the cadet had managed to get for him by shouting a few orders to his junior cadets, Menon walked up the stairs to meet other officers. As he entered the massive hall, he found cadets sitting in batches, with the instructional staff imparting training to cadets on their respective subjects.

Menon met Col Murugan, the officer in charge of training the group contingent for the competition. An officer with good knowledge of NCC, this being his third tenure with the organisation, Col Murugan told Menon enthusiastically about the meticulous planning that he had carried out to train the cadets to ensure a good performance in the competition. He also told that the "Best Cadet" event was a last-minute inclusion in the "Thal Sainik Camp" competition by the NCC HQs at New Delhi, which was otherwise held only during the more glamorous "Republic Day Camp". He also mentioned to Menon, that everyone expects only a token participation by the group team in the "Best Cadet" event as Cadets from the colleges in the Group's area of responsibility weren't considered up to the mark for the competition as compared to the cadets from prestigious colleges of Chennai and Coimbatore. He tried to sugarcoat his statement by explaining that the strong point of the cadets of their group, which both these officers were part of, was their physical abilities and were therefore expected to do better in events where brawns took priority over brains.

"I don't accept", Menon muttered to himself. Menon had learnt this technique from one of the monks that he had interacted with while he was posted to Myanmar at the Defence Services Academy of Myanmar army. During his conversations with the monk, Menon observed that after every few sentences, the monk used to say " I accept" or "I don't accept" with absolute serenity on his face. After a few days when Menon couldn't hold back the curiosity, he asked the monk for the reason. The monk said "We need to give regular commands to our brain and mind. Without our commands, the brain will take anything that is fed to it and accept anything that gives immediate gratification without considering long-term effects. Unless we keep our mind under a tight leash with regular and assertive commands, it can take one on disastrous paths". Menon had liked the idea, and though he couldn't gather the courage to imitate the monk fully by telling the commands loudly in front of others, he made it a point to give silent commands to his minds during conversations so that the mind doesn't accept things that weren't good for him in the long term. And today during his conversation with Col Murugan, it was important not to accept certain opinions that Col Murugan was giving about the Cadets of Madurai group. It was important for Menon not to accept the opinion if he wanted to train the cadets for the "Best Cadet" event on an optimistic note and make his training purposeful. He knew it very well that if "hope" becomes the first casualty in any endeavour then the entire journey becomes meaningless. On the other hand, if any endeavour is taken while being optimistic about success, even if the desired results are not achieved, it leads to intangible achievements which last longer than the goals themselves that are sought to be achieved. He had great conviction in the fact that the changes that are brought in a person while trying to achieve goals were more important than the achievement of the goal itself. The process was more important than the product, but the process had to be carried out with the conviction that the desired product would be attained and then it didn't matter whether the achievement was made or not. The persistent, passionate process towards attaining it is what will change a person and not the attainment of the goal. Make a strong purpose, and focus only on the process without bothering if the goal is achieved or not. While following any process with intensity and faith, it no longer matters whether the goal is achieved or not, and it is the only foolproof method to achieve any desired goal. The irony of the philosophy was intriguing; focus on the process alone and the realisation of the product will be nothing but a certainty and that was a universal truth. Difficult to understand, but once understood gives a person absolute freedom from attachment to the outcome. Years back when Menon had come across this Shloka from Gita

$$\text{कर्मण्येवाधिकारस्ते मा फलेषु कदाचन।}$$
$$\text{मा कर्मफलहेतुर्भुर्मा ते संगोऽस्त्वकर्मणि॥}$$

he had not been able to make complete sense of the message, of detachment that one must have to the outcome, that these verses were trying to convey, but today he was able to understand it in its entirety. As the thoughts flew like sparks inside the optimistic circuitry inside his brain he muttered once again " I don't accept". This time with greater conviction than before. He took a quick look around, disconnecting his eye contact with Col Murugan. The day looked brighter, the air was filled with a strange fragrance of hopefulness. Menon said thanks to Col Murugan for the brief that was provided on the preparation of cadets, he acknowledged the fine details that Col Murugan had gone into while discussing the events and while talking about his plans for winning the Inter Group competition. Making a mental note of this quality and promising himself that he too would try to follow it, he went to observe the cadets who were in the respective syndicates preparing for the events that they had volunteered for and were now shortlisted. When he was being assigned the task, his superior officer had told him to pick up cadets for the 'Best Cadet' from other events since there were quite many spare cadets to meet contingencies. Menon moved from one class to another, hoping to get a general level of the cadets. Some of them were his cadets from Tirunelveli and adjoining areas. Since it was mostly a monologue being delivered by the instructors, and there was little interaction between the cadets and the instructor, he found it difficult to gauge even a rough estimate of the level of cadets to assess their suitability to compete in the 'Best Cadet' category. The duty- NCO blew the whistle to announce the termination of classes scheduled in the morning session. It was also the lunch break, therefore Menon got up and went to the dining hall where he met Col Murugan again. He also met other officers who had been made in charge of training the cadets for various events of TSC. Under the watch of Col Murugan, the training had been very well organised wherein Col Murugan himself was overall in charge of the training with other officers responsible for the sub-events of the competition. Menon came to know that the Group Commander while giving freedom of action to his officers, was a regular visitor to the training area to take stock of the progress and to facilitate easing out the bottlenecks. Menon, during the conversations while having lunch, asked Col Murugan if he could meet all the Cadets so that he could choose the probable ones who could be fielded for the " Best Cadet" category. Col Murugan agreed to the suggestion and he passed orders for organising the same at 5 PM the same day in the auditorium. Menon went back to his room for his afternoon siesta, with not even a little inkling of the rollercoaster ride of emotions that he was going to go through in the next few months. He was unaware of the momentous occasions that he was going to witness. He from the position of being a Commanding Officer was going to be humbled by the enormous resilience, tolerance to pain, and steadfastness that he was going to witness amongst the Cadets whom he was tasked to train. He was soon going to experience a paradigm shift in how he had always perceived NCC to be. From being an organisation where the work involved wasn't considered to be anywhere near real soldiering, he would perceive it to be one that would reveal to him his life's purpose. He was going to experience the joy of a unique kind, unexplainable, blissful. And more than joy he was going to be cocooned for a considerable time in a world which contained only the elements of hard work, persistence, grit, sweat, toil, inspiration, ambition, tears of success and stains of dried-up tears indicating the transition from despondency to determination. His amygdala, the seat of emotions in the brain, was going to be bombarded with myriad emotions of great degree. He was going to experience the ecstasy of being in a flow, the bliss of deep work. If Paradise is a place where one experiences nothing but ecstasy, then he was soon going to experience that. But for then, he had drifted off to sleep with questions in his mind on the very basic issue of how he was going to get his pick of cadets to train them for the competition.

"Excuse me, sir, I have a doubt regarding this question". Menon was briefly interrupted in his nostalgic rumination by a cadet. He lumbered towards him and cleared his doubt. He took a look around and found others to be deeply involved in their efforts to attempt the questions in the paper given to them. He came back to his chair and tried to recollect the point at which his chain of thoughts was interrupted. He took some time to join the threads of his reverie and very soon he resumed his journey into the past.

Col Murugan, on Menon's request, had passed orders for the Cadets to be assembled at 5 PM, in the auditorium so that Menon could pick the cadets to be trained for the "Best Cadet" category. As he climbed on the dias and looked at the cadets who were seated in neat rows in the hall. The girl cadets were seated on to his right and the boys were on his left. Since the stage on which he was standing was raised reasonably high, the cadets had to look up to face him. As he tried to screen the gathering to get some superficial data, he found that a few were looking at him with intense curiosity, while a few had decided not to take the trouble of looking up and had kept the gaze parallel or down towards the floor. Could he take that as a sign of interest and indifference? Being an assessor, while Menon had become adept at identifying body language, he also was quite cautious in making hasty conclusions. He decided to start with the girl cadets. And at that very moment, he realised that it wasn't his decision. It was a decision by his unconscious mind. He had always been a "RIGHT" person. He invariably wore his shoes always on his right foot first. He shaved the right side of his face first. If there were two doors to a hall, he used the right one. His brain circuit was oriented towards taking a direction towards the right. It was reassuring and scary at the same time to realise the grip habits have on our lives. It's only in the first few occasions that an action is taken from the conscious level, with time it gets controlled from subconscious and unconscious levels once it becomes a habit. These habits have such strong control over our selves that it becomes difficult to break free from them even when one wants to. No wonder, that a smoker, even after being advised by the doctor not to smoke since his reports suggest his proneness to lung cancer, on a slight excuse, reaches for the poison stick despite being fully aware of the grave consequences.

Back then, he decided to go with his habit of looking at the right side, since that was a natural habit. He asked for volunteers among the girl cadets for the "Best Cadet" event. But before doing that, he had explained the sub-events in the category and certain requirements that the cadets must possess like communication skills, the ability to grasp and put effort into studying the service subjects etc. He had asked for the first 10 volunteers. He had specified a number as he wanted those who would make decisions fast and who were ready to take the initiative. As the volunteer cadets stood up and started moving towards the stage he found that the majority of them were the ones who were looking at him with interest and curiosity and it was very few of those who had sat there with their gaze towards the floor. He scanned the lot in front of him. From the vantage point, he was able to observe the body language of the cadets. He had noticed a cadet who was wearing an appointment badge of 'Senior Under Officer' with a smart bearing and pleasing appearance. The combination of appearance and the fact that she was also an appointment, hence her likelihood of doing well in NCC, made Menon hope that she would volunteer for the event. He looked behind him on the stage and found that there were already 10 volunteer cadets. "Maybe a little prodding might get her to volunteer", he thought. "Ok, I will take one more cadet", he said, this time keeping his gaze on the Senior Under Officer. Two hands rose from the front row. Both were ordinary cadets with no epaulette of rank on their shoulders. He let the decision hang in the air for a moment, hoping that this silence would make the SUO raise her hand as well. He saw her talking to the cadet sitting by her side. Menon was hopeful. He wanted to give her some more time to decide. Since he could not prolong the suspense any longer he had to give a decision to the two cadets who had raised their hands 'Anyone from the two of you', Menon addressed the two volunteers from the front row. They both were standing. As the two cadets looked at each other, the shorter cadets signalled the taller one to proceed. Menon, though observed the actions, it didn't interest him much as he had been wanting the SUO to volunteer. The taller one moved to the stage. 'One last try' Menon thought. 'I will take one more volunteer', he said, now with a bit of frustration for not being able to achieve his objective of prodding the SUO to volunteer. And to his big disappointment the shorter girl from the front row who had allowed the other cadet to move to the stage a few seconds earlier, got up and walked to the stage. Menon took a hard look at the cadet who had not let his last attempt have its full effect. The cadet walking to the stage was just about 5 feet tall, an ordinary cadet, nothing unique about her, a very ordinary cadet. The SUO was still busy whispering to her neighbour, with absolutely no intention of volunteering. Menon gave up and looked behind him. There were 12 cadets with the last cadet just joining the group. He scanned the 'dozen' and felt a sense of disappointment growing inside him, for none of them displayed body language of confidence or intense desire to participate in the event. The last cadet who had joined the group was standing a little away from the group, the gap between her and the neighbouring cadet slightly more than the gap other cadets had maintained with each other. Menon didn't want to waste his time on her. He took a deep breath to accept the situation that his 'Best Cadet' would have to come from this lot that was standing in front of him. The deep breath helped him regain his composure and also infuse fresh optimism into his mind which had been dealing with frustration for his failure of getting the "SUO" to volunteer for the event. He wanted to check them for their communication skills, spontaneity in thinking, logicality, confidence in putting across their point of view and courage to initiate and sustain.

He threw a topic for them to discuss " *Who or what do you take recourse to while facing a problem?" and he gave them three leads, "Parents", "Friends" or "Your Diary"?* The cadets started coming out with their points. Menon found the points routine and quite ordinary, nothing close to what is expected from a potential best cadet. The points being provided were more emotional based, personal, conservative and following a societal mindset rather than being rational. "Our parents are like gods, they only wish good for us, hence we should approach only them for our problems," said one of the best cadet aspirants. The manner in which the point was being put across was so superficial that it didn't require too much intelligence to conclude that this cadet would hardly be listening to what her parents told her, let alone putting them on such a high pedestal that she was now professing. And more importantly, can the intention of goodness alone solve the problems? What about the capacity, skill and knowledge required to solve the problems? What about the generation gap, the differing mindset on social concepts, and the fact that some of the parents would not even have seen a college? Won't all that prevent them from solving all the problems of their child despite having the right intention? Similar points were brought in favour of the second lead of 'friends' as well. Menon was losing the confidence in the cadets on the stage and was about to put the discussion open to the audience hoping to see some spark from them, when he heard a faint voice trying to make itself heard. *"Sir, I always take recourse to write down my problems in my diary, because at times my parents or friends may not be able to correctly appreciate my situation and therefore may not be able to give the right advice. But when I write my problem in my diary I can deliberate on it in a better way and I believe that solutions to our problems lie within us. We just need to look harder. The diary makes me look harder into myself and I get the solution".* Menon was awestruck, not just because what he heard was logical, pragmatic, strong and filled with self-belief, but also because of where it came from. It was the 12th cadet, the 5-foot girl, who had got onto the stage not due to any assessment prowess of Menon, but due to an act of pure providence. She wasn't looking into the air, or gazing to the ground, but had maintained a firm eye contact with Menon. There was an air of self-assured confidence. Menon looked at the SUO who was busy talking to the cadet next to her and then he quickly shifted to the girl who had spoken such strong words. He felt elated and miserable at the same time. It's intriguing how two opposing emotions can be experienced by a human at the same time. Tears of joy, the sheepish smile of embarrassment, fear and courage emerging simultaneously are a few of the instances when the duality of emotions occurs inside the human mind. Menon was ecstatic about being able to get his best cadet, but he was feeling miserable for letting his assessment be dominated by external appearance. Despite his years of experience in the assessment system, where he had to daily protect himself against the halo/horn effect, he had let this bias cloud his assessment. But at that time his sense of relief and excitement at finding the cadet who met his expected requirements and with necessary attributes to become a strong contender for the event had overtaken the emotions of feeling miserable at the lapse he made in his judgement. He quickly gave another topic for discussion so that he could get a reserve girl cadet for the event. Since he had strongly made up his mind on whom he was going to focus on during training and whom he was going to field in the best Girl cadet category, he felt pangs of guilt for the cadets whom he took as reserve. But he took solace in the quote " What you become while trying to achieve something is much more important than your achievement itself". He was sure that the cadets chosen as a reserve would also enrich and enhance her personality attributes by the end of the training. Not in this instance, but events later in his tenure in NCC were going to prove to him that one must never write off the reserve cadet, for, one never knows who might spring a surprise. The human mind works in strange ways. At what point, by what event can the mind change its perception, one could never know. And that change alters the actions that the mind commands which in turn changes a person completely. Such is the potential of humans and a tiny spark can arouse it to blossom to its full realisation. While Menon had heard and even read about it, the events that he was destined to experience would bring him face to face with the ultimate potential that a human being could possess. Through the path of struggles and tears, he was soon going to experience the bliss of witnessing the breaking of perceived limits. He was going to witness the victory of belief over circumstances. His perception that a reserve was meant to be only that was going to be broken. But in this instance, the cadet selected serendipitously would be the one who would go all the way and bring name and fame to herself and to all who were associated with her. Menon looked at her with the joy that one probably finds at the end of a treasure hunt. Her name was Rashi Kripa and she was a native of *Marthandam,* a little-known place near the tip of the bottommost district of India-Kanyakumari

Now it was time to select the cadet from the boys for the event. To his shock, he found that there were hardly any volunteers among the boys. "Was Col Murugan right?" Menon remembered the conversation that he had with the officer in charge of training the group TSC contingent. He tried to quickly remove any defeatist thoughts coming his way. And as he tried to do that, he wondered "Where is Mahesh?". He must have spoken it out loudly, for one of his fellow cadets informed him that Cadet Mahesh had to go to his house to attend a family function and may not be available for the rest of the camp. Menon carried out the selection of boy cadets in a perfunctory manner by nominating a few cadets who came up reluctantly for the selection. But despite the non-interest shown by the cadets Menon's mood was upbeat, he knew that he had already found his best cadet among the boys. He wrapped up the selection process, instructed a senior cadet to make a written list of the selected cadets and submit the same to him in his office and left the stage. He immediately got hold of cadet Mahesh's phone number and gave him a call. During the talk, Mahesh told him that while he was eager to give it a try, his father had some apprehension about the impact that it would have on his studies. Menon understood the concern very well. A cadet has to make a trade-off between the benefits that he could accrue from the NCC activities versus the impact that it could have on his/her academic performance. Both Mahesh and his father came to the campsite the next day and it took some amount of persuasion to convince his father to allow him to participate in the event.

Chapter 3

Setting Up the Arena

Having got the pupil of his choice, Menon immediately got into the preparation for commencing their training for the event. Best Cadet event in TSC consists of multiple sub-events like assessment of NCC subject knowledge and general awareness, firing skills, military drill and above all, the personality assessment which includes personality interview and certain activities to be done in a group like delivering a lecturette and group discussion. These tests and assessments aim to elicit and measure the personality attributes of the cadets participating in the event. He had to get them battle-ready in 30 days i.e. in 3 camps of 10 days duration each. He had identified two aspects that he had to tackle. One was of course the syllabus and activities that constituted the sub-events and the more important second one was the building of a winner's mindset in these cadets.

Collecting the resources was the first step in preparation. He went through the instructions on the event that were received from the superior headquarters that was responsible for the conduct of the event. He wrote down meticulously all the rules and regulations and important highlights regarding each event. He photocopied all the important instructions and neatly pinned them in a file for referring them in the days to come so that he wouldn't waste his time either asking others or searching for them in the disorganised almirah of the training clerk. After that he got the latest NCC manuals downloaded from an authentic site and got sufficient copies printed. While there was an option of sending soft copies to the cadets through mail and other technological platforms, Menon always preferred the hard copies. If one uses mobile phones for carrying softcopies and reading from them, then one is prone to external distractions like phone calls and also by forces of habit where one is likely to drift towards social media distractions. He had learnt that one way to reduce distraction and remain focussed on the job is to keep the distraction at a sufficient distance where it becomes inconvenient to reach. Secondly, a personal hard copy of the manual gives the freedom for more intimate interaction with the book. One can underline, highlight, write side notes etc which is not feasible in a soft copy. Next, he downloaded month-wise summary of all important events in politics, sports and science and technology both at the national and international levels for preparing the cadets for the general knowledge assessment. Having been a Group Testing Officer, he had his templates for personality assessment of cadets. He spoke to the officer who was in charge of firing, to coordinate the timings for firing practice by the "Best Cadets". He coordinated with Col Murugan for the provisioning of target papers and ammunition for firing, stationary for setting question papers, answer sheets etc and of course a table and chair for him to set up his office. He then sat down to take a deep breath. He knew the perils of sudden excitement and its effect on decision-making. Any surge in emotion whether positive or negative has a definite impact on the rational part of the brain. Any decision taken with an overwhelming component of emotions makes one take decisions which either don't last long or prove detrimental in the long run. He understood very well the role of emotions. They put you on the right track as they are aligned with your values, desires and dreams. But once given the direction by emotions, the rational mind must take over to traverse the rest of the journey. He had also experienced the negative impact of being overwhelmed when one tries to perceive and tackle a situation as a whole. He reaffirmed to himself the principle of atomisation of a given task and not to underestimate the importance of small steps. The only way to tackle any situation is to atomise and break a larger problem into smaller manageable problems. Just like a marathon runner; even while the runner needs to keep the final destination in mind, he must keep his focus on the immediate next step, which should be sure and firm. It is the "Now" that has the power to craft the "Future". Once he had gone over his guiding philosophies, which he often reminded himself by going over them occasionally from the notes he had stored in his phone, he was mentally ready for the task. Menon believed that every person must live by following the mantras, that he/she closely associates with. These mantras are like the rudder of a boat, they help in maintaining the direction of one's life.

Having collected the material resources and also preparing himself mentally for the impending responsibility, he now decided to set up his training team. While he decided to take on the responsibility of training the cadets for the sub-events like preparation of NCC subjects and personality assessment, he needed subject matter experts on drill, firing and someone to assist in covering the general knowledge portion for all the months starting from 1st of January till date. His experience in the armed forces had made him wiser on the concept of decentralisation and delegation. He was quite conscious of the fact that he should bite only what he could chew. While inspecting the various activities going on in the camp, he observed a Non-Commissioned Officer, *Hav Murugan.* The NCO was quite calm and was also qualified in the military drill course. More than the skill that he had acquired during the drill, he was quite adept at understanding the shortcomings of his mentees and providing appropriate advice to the cadets to overcome them. While Menon had observed that most of the drill instructors were only yelling out the faults of the cadets, it was *Murugan* who was instructing correction along with calling out the faults. He observed that Murugan spent considerable time giving exercises to the cadets on various aspects rather than making them do multiple cycles of drill. Probably he had understood a basic philosophy that is responsible for our successes and failures, which is " You become perfect at what you keep doing repeatedly". He knew that if he made the cadets practice without removing their shortcomings, they would only become perfect in what they were practising, and without removing the errors, the cadets were simply repeating their shortcomings. Due to his short height and not-so-commanding tone, other NCOs who were loud, indulged in theatrics and displayed better energy were preferred over him. Col Murugan, was joyfully surprised when Menon had put in a request to him for allotting Hav Murugan the responsibility of training the "Best Cadets" on military drills. NCC as an organisation is staffed with a limited number of defence personnel, and it is rare to find personnel who are qualified in skills like firing, drill etc as the regular army units hesitate to send them out of their units due to their obvious utility in unit affairs. Also, it was seen that a person who was good in say firing or drill was found to be good in other fields too which is not surprising as it is said "Excellence is not an act but a habit". Col Murugan, was happy that Menon was not another contender for more sought-after drill instructors available in the group.

Having settled the issue of drill instructor, Menon now had to look for an *Associate NCC Officer*, who could help him with the training of cadets on the General Knowledge. For those who are unversed with this terminology, ANOs are the teachers or professors of a school or college who volunteer to be part of NCC, go through a short course in NCC training and get commissioned as officers. Keeping their academic qualifications in perspective and their job as teachers, these ANOs even though junior in ranks they wear on their shoulders are given the due respect by the regular officers of the armed forces. So it isn't rare or considered out of place to see a Colonel or an officer of higher rank addressing an ANO who was a Lieutenant as 'Sir' or 'Maam". The highest rank that an ANO could expect to rise to is that of the rank of 'Major'. A few of them take their job very seriously and are instrumental in not just running the NCC unit in their institutions effectively but are also an inspiring figure for the cadets. A few others are more interested in the perks that they received as a privilege of becoming an ANO. Getting an ANO with a good work ethic and a favourable attitude towards the welfare of cadets was essential for the task of training the Best Cadets. An NCC camp in Tamilnadu Directorate is authorised eight ANOs. Menon decided to have a close observation of their behaviour, the way they carried out the tasks allotted to them and also their casual conversations. And while doing that he came across Lieutenant Hemalaxmi, an ANO from an

Engineering college at *Kovilpatti*. Lt Hemalaxmi was a lady with a calm demeanour yet very effective when it came to dealing with the cadets. Her tone of voice was strict and yet reassuring at the same time. She never displayed frustration even when the mischievous cadets went overboard with their antics. It was like she knew where exactly the harmless mischiefs ended and where it could become detrimental for the cadets themselves and others. Menon found that, unlike others, she utilised the breaks in training not to get away from something that she considered to be dreary and a responsibility that she had to somehow get done with, but he found that she always came back from the breaks with the same enthusiasm and joy that she had gone for the break with. Her actions and motivation, made Menon introspect his own sense of commitment to the work that he was assigned with and promised himself to catch up with her dedication. She would show the same dedication even in tasks where she wasn't assigned the sole responsibility for a particular task and hence also would not have been solely credited for the accomplishment of the same.

"Ma'am, would you like to be part of the team training the Best Cadets of the group for the forthcoming Inter Group Competition for TSC?", Menon asked her. "Sir, I don't know much about it, but if it is challenging enough and can teach me something new, I will be quite willing for the same. But before committing I would also like to ask for the permission of my commanding

Officer and my College to attend the same", she replied with that ever-present serene smile on her face. At that moment, Menon knew that the universe was planning something significant for him. Everything seemed to be falling into place. The cadets whom he never knew, but perfectly fit in with his expectations, the drill instructor with all the qualities that he was looking for and now this ANO being present in this camp. In her conversations, the ANO had not just displayed her desire to take on challenges in life but also displayed her inclination to take deliberate decisions, devoid of impulsivity, and after due consultation with her superiors both in her NCC unit and her institution. Her ability to make mature decisions coupled with her sense of responsibility and effective functioning in dealing with the cadets made her an appropriate candidate to be part of the training team that Menon was looking to set up. Giving a silent word of thanks to the universe, he proceeded to call up the Commanding Officer of the ANO to seek his permission to include his ANO in the training team for training the Best Cadets.

Chapter 4

The Steady Grind to Transformation

Menon was an early riser and the day the training was to start was a special day for Menon. He was up by 3 AM. There was a mix of enthusiasm and nervousness that he was experiencing since the time he woke up. The way things were falling into place had increased his positive expectancy towards the outcome of the efforts that he and the cadets were going to invest in the next few weeks. While positive expectancy is a result of various factors like deliberate planning, acquiring of required skills, consistency, and persistence, there was a significant factor that helped in acquiring a mindset of positive expectancy. He had chanced upon this factor as a common philosophy that he had found in most of the personality development books that he had been reading. Over a while, he had become quite convinced about its universal applicability. For any objective to be achieved in physical reality, it should have already been imagined as having been achieved in one's mind. As Napolean Hill has stated, "What your mind can conceive and believe, it can achieve". It is this repeated focus on our objective that starts creating a positive expectancy towards the achievement of the same. When we send repeated thoughts of a particular nature to our mind, the mind, acting like a sounding board, reflects it, in a clearer and louder manner, back to us. And it doesn't judge, it reflects, without bias or prejudice for or against any thoughts. It simply reflects.

With the joyful positive expectancy in mind, he sat down for meditation and also to carry out affirmation and visualisation of the achievement of the objective that he had set for himself. Against the backdrop of soothing instrumental meditation music, he was soon drawn into a relaxed world of mindfulness. He was aware of his deep synchronous breathing. He could feel his shoulder muscles losing the tension, his spine becoming supple, and his breathing become more rhythmic, slow and deep. The cacophony of the mindless chatter in his head was being subsumed by the nothingness that had started engulfing him. Even in that state, there was a tiny element of conscious awareness making him realise that his mind was being drained of the disorganised and purposeless thoughts and making it ready to receive the commands that he was going to give. As he delved deeper into the nothingness, he could feel his cells aligned together in one direction, just like the particles of a magnet, and he was ready to attract to his life what he desired. He commanded his mind to see in every detail the path that would be forged towards the achievement of the objective as well as its accomplishment. He saw the classes being taken, the regular assessment of the cadets in various sub-events and how each time they performed well on it. He visualised them doing perfect drills, firing every bullet on the target and speaking confidently during the personal interview and the group discussions. As his mind conceived the fructification of his endeavour in his mind, he could feel a bout of energy flowing through his body. As he opened his eyes, he could feel the difference in the space surrounding him. It was brighter, hopeful and above all it was filled with serenity of unexplainable level. But in reality the surroundings had not changed, it was his inner space that had become organised and was devoid of clutter. As you are within so you are without. Menon wondered if the difference he was finding in his surroundings was due to the breaking out of dawn or was it because the clouds of self-doubt and apprehension had been swept away by the gush of positivity through the meditational process that he had just practised. He took a look around his room to check if everything was in order, stepped out of the door and walked towards the hall where he had asked the Best Cadets to gather. He felt different. The steps were firmer, the head was tilted up, the shoulders were stretched back and his mood was of supreme confidence. One's posture and gait were a result of the feelings and emotions that were going on inside him. And there indeed is another related corollary, that the gait and posture influence the state one is in. If one is sad and decides to look up rather than stare at the floor, it changes the state that one is to a certain extent. The way the mind and body work in synchronicity with each other, the mind starts associating certain postures with specific feelings and emotions.

As he entered the hall where the cadets were seated, he found Rashi and Mahesh to be sitting on the front row. They had not disappointed him. The eagerness to learn, the enthusiasm to face something new and purposeful, that he had expected from them was visible in the fact that the two had decided to occupy the front row. Apart from these two cadets, there were others whom he had selected to get a viable group for training.

He felt that this would make the training more effective because of the competition that a cadet perceives from other cadets. While overall these cadets didn't fit the requirement, each had his/her unique capability. Some were good in drill, some in firing and some in their communication skills. Menon had deliberately kept these cadets in the group of best cadets to establish a benchmark to which he expected Aswin and Mahesh to reach. Most of these cadets were not volunteers as they had wished to participate in other events of TSC. Col Murugan had coordinated with Menon to ensure that these cadets got an opportunity to practice and get selected for the event that they were interested in while being part of the Best Cadet group.

Sitting among them was also a cadet from his unit, cadet Saraswathi. Menon had discovered Saraswathy, during the Annual Training Camp of his unit. He had found her to be gritty, ambitious and willing to face challenges. Despite her petite figure, Saraswathy had been excellent on the Obstacle course and was selected for the group team and was at *Idiyappatti* for further training. By her attitude she would have perfectly met the requirements of the best cadet except that, being from the remote town of Tirunelveli, she was restricted in the use of the English language. While Menon was sure that he wouldn't be able to enhance her English language proficiency in the given time, he wanted her to realise her shortcomings so that she would work on them in the future. Menon was sure that Saraswathy was the type of person who could create and sustain her flame of personal growth by the spark of realisation given to her by external means. She too was one of the non-volunteers sitting with visible discomfort. " It is this discomfort, that will make her grow. Like they say, you don't become strong despite the storm but because of it", Menon said to himself, taking satisfaction at the discomfort that the cadet was facing. Had she been indifferent, it would have negated the objective that he had for her. Menon, even while being optimistic about the results of the effort, held more dearly the philosophies that he had for living life. And one of his philosophies relevant to the present context was that, it was not the achievement of a goal that was important, but what you become while trying to achieve it". And it was based on this philosophy that he had put Saraswathy in a position of discomfort.

Desire and Faith

With a final glance at the gathering of cadets, he started with the presentation that he had prepared on the methodology that he was going to adopt for training the best cadets. He flashed the first slide on the screen, it had two words written on it, DESIRE and FAITH. As Menon immersed himself in these two words, he could experience a strange kind of strength entering his body. That's the power of mantras that you live by. He had acknowledged the power of these two words as one of the ultimate truth. His conviction in the power of these two words arose both because he had read it as the experience of some of the greats in different walks of life, like athletes, artists, teachers, entrepreneurs, politicians and many more, and also since he had experienced it himself. He believed it to such an extent, that whenever he failed to achieve a set objective, he always questioned either his desire or the belief that he had in carrying out the task, and tried to not hold the external circumstances or limiting conditions that he may have faced as the possible reason. While 'ego' always tries to protect one from the impact of failure by looking for external reasons, real growth occurs only when one holds oneself responsible. Questioning one's desire or faith in the event of non-achievement of a set objective, made one responsible for it. And when one is responsible for an outcome, he/she also retains the power to change or modify the same. After all, responsibility stands for "ability to respond". When one takes responsibility for the consequences or outcomes then one sees failure not as something which defines them but as something that occurred due to factors which can be changed and within the control of the individual. Menon now had to put across these ideas in an impactful manner. If the cadets can understand and assimilate the importance of these two factors of desire and faith, they will become a significant driving force towards their dreams. He had to be dramatic. He tilted his body to one side and spread his arms on either side. The cadets, who were looking forward enthusiastically to the schedule and methods to be employed for training, gave a perplexed look.

"ITNI SHIDDATH SE TUMKO PANEY KI KOSHISH KI HAI, KI HAR ZARRE NE TUMSEY MILANEY KI SAAJISH KI HAI".

As Menon spoke these lines from a Bollywood movie, almost as if chanting a mantra, he could see a flicker of excitement on the faces staring at him. One odd cadet from the northern part of India had tried to whisper these lines along with him. The majority of the Tamil-speaking cadets were waiting for the translation of lines which must have appealed to their auditory sense since most of them were wearing an inquisitive smile. Menon continued, with passion and emotions gripping every word that was coming out of his mouth. " When you desire something from your heart, and when you can think of nothing but about your desire, then all the elements of the universe come together, not just to help you…", he paused to let it settle down, lowered his tone as if going to say a secret, "but to *conspire* together to help you to achieve it". He stopped to feel the gush of energy that these lines had always sent through his veins. He could feel the veins in his temples stiffening, he was using every amount of his willpower to keep his emotions under control. Emotions that are taken to a peak and held at that place for a few moments have a better impact than the ones where it is let go. "And what happens if despite your intense desire and consequent hard work you still don't achieve it?". Now there was no one gazing at the floor. Everyone in the hall was waiting for the answer as it affected them all. "We all are, in some way searching for answers", Menon's soliloquy was too softly done to be heard by anyone except by himself who heard it quite loudly. Menon continued in a very deliberate manner "Everyone present here knows that there are a limited number of vacancies for each event. And it's only a few of you who will make it to the final list. Does it mean that the law of desire doesn't work for others? No. For others, the same law works differently. When despite your intense desire and focussed work you don't attain what you desire, then the universe gifts you with what you deserve". Menon smiled at the anticipated disappointment that swept across some of the faces. It is quite natural for us to think that we don't deserve much. That's the mindset that most of us have been conditioned to. We feel we are not worth much. So desires are always held higher than what we feel we deserve. Today was the day to break that mindset. "When you have invested your soul in what you desire and still don't get it, the universe sends you what you deserve. "And the fact is that', Menon paused, before speaking the next few words, to have its required impact. He then continued "in such a situation what you deserve will be much better and bigger than what you had desired". The gazes had become more intense and he could feel the urge for more in those eyes. He continued "Girls and boys, these are universal truths that have stood the test of time. These have been relevant all times that was and for all the times that are to come". A question flashed across his mind wondering if he was speaking like a modern-day spiritual guru. Though he was speaking from his conviction, he didn't want to go overboard either with his intonation or with his gestures. But then it occurred to him that it indeed was a spiritual journey that each one of them was going to embark upon. He as the mentor and they as students, were going to face their demons and also get enlightened about the abilities that they have been gifted with. A journey where the self was unravelled had to be a spiritual journey. Menon could feel the joy of the paradigm shift in perception. He was now perceiving the event not as a competition with others but as a journey of self-discovery and self-growth. There was no fear about the results, neither was there any kind of negative feeling towards the competitors. Menon had not realised it, but unwittingly he had given these cadets a very important success formula which was that success comes to those who are focussed and oriented inwards, those who are devoted to and busy taking actions to reach their highest level of performance without bothering about external circumstances, including the competitors. It is in this state of flow that the miracles occur. And Menon and his cadets were going to witness miracles that Tamilnadu Directorate had not seen for a while.

Having prepped the cadets mentally for the event, Menon went about the schedule that he had planned for each day. The morning was to start with five minutes of meditation and affirmation about the belief in their ability to achieve their objective to program their subconscious mind to transform the thoughts to reality, then there was a josh run and stretching to wake up the body from slumber and to get the dose of dopamine in the correct way to remain energised for the rest of the day. After an hour's break which included the time to shower and have breakfast, they had to gather at the drill square to be mentored by *Hav Murugan* on the nuances of drill. The forty minutes of intense drill practice was to be followed by classes on service subjects. In the thirty days of three camps, of ten days each, available to them, Menon had planned the schedule in such a manner that the first camp was meant to provide conceptual clarity to the cadets on various topics of the service (NCC) subjects, the next two camps were meant only to assess the knowledge and conceptual clarity gained by the cadets, to make them familiar with the questions and remove the fear of exams.

One of the unique and surprising facts about the mind is that it doesn't crave happiness or motivation, it only craves familiarity. One needs to fall in love with doing something which may be boring but is important. Despite the feeling of being bored when one repeats it continuously to such an extent that it becomes familiar to the mind, it no longer takes any effort for the mind to look forward to doing the same again and again. Discipline and willpower help you to make the actions, that are important to you, familiar to your mind. Once they become familiar it takes less and less effort to keep going back to do it repeatedly irrespective of how you would have felt the first time when the task was encountered. The mind can't discriminate between good and bad. It doesn't discriminate between smoking, checking social media or going for a jog. Whatever is familiar, it will crave for it and drive you towards doing it. And Menon, wanted his cadets to be familiar with exam pattern, the drill movements and answering questions in an interview to such an extent that the mind becomes familiar with it. At noon, the cadets were to attend firing at the *short range(a 50 m firing range)* under the officer in charge of firing. Menon had planned to attend this activity, despite not being in charge of it, because the behaviour and performance of a person at the firing range told a lot about his/her personality. It was also a place quite suited to change the perception and make a paradigm shift in the mindset, which was the ultimate end that Menon was aiming at.

The post-lunch session was dedicated to enhancing General Knowledge. This was to be handled by Lt Hemalakshmi who would have had the time in the morning to prepare for the same. There was an agenda of self-interest in such scheduling as it helped Menon to get his favourite afternoon siesta. He could utilise this time to also set the question paper for the daily evening assessment. After the evening tea and a break of one hour, the cadets were to gather for the personality assessment session in which Menon had planned to conduct group discussions, lecturettes, mock interviews etc. After the dinner break, the cadets had to go through the daily written exam and that was to be followed by a meditation session in the open ground before they retired for a well-deserved sleep. He announced that the schedule was to be followed with immediate effect. Since the time for the run, that day was taken up by the briefing. the cadets now had to gather at the drill ground after having a shower and breakfast.

Menon was at the drill ground at sharp 8 AM, and so was the drill instructor. The cadets were not yet there. As the cadets filled in, Hav Murugan, sent them on a round around the drill square. It served both as a punishment for the cadets for coming late and also to warm them up for the drill session. "If you feel having your *Idlis* are more important than reaching the drill ground on time, then you are average cadets not best cadets, because that's what an average cadet does", Murugan spoke in a calm but stinging tone. "You always have a choice and the choices that you give importance to will dictate the results. Don't waste your tears after the time for preparation has been wasted". The *NCO* who had not even completed his higher secondary school had uttered the time-tested philosophy of life. One doesn't need to read books or go to school and just keeping ones' senses open to absorb experiences is enough to be enlightened about the eternal philosophies of life. Hav Murugan, Menon noted, was not a man in a hurry. Complimenting his composed manner of conversation was the deliberate manner in which he tackled a given task. While he was not tall and neither did he have a good military bearing, and therefore never got recognised as a good instructor. But he had all the making of a *Ustaad.* On the first day, he gave a short briefing on the drill and what was expected of the best cadets in the drill ground. " Drill is all about *Waqfa* and *Nakhra",* he said. And in those words, he had brought out the essence of what can be called a good drill. The *Waqfa or the* pauses that you give between the various actions and the *Nakhra* or the style with which you display and act out various postures is what makes a good drill. The first day was spent on arms exercises. All the cadets were made to stand with bricks in their hands and made to swing to and fro. This was done to loosen the shoulder muscles so that, the arm swing, which is an essential aspect of good drill is improved. After 30 mins of this activity, he made each one of them keep their right leg on a raised platform in a manner that the entire leg was parallel to the ground. Thereafter he asked them to put the force using the entire leg downwards. This exercise was required to help the cadets to loosen the muscles at the hip joint just like how the earlier exercise was meant to loosen the shoulder muscles. This would help the cadets to move their legs freely while marching and help them to take the leg as high as possible, which was another criterion of a good drill. The cadets who were looking forward to marching and other activities associated with drill were evidently disappointed. After some time they seemed to be getting bored with the monotonous exercise routine that they were being subjected to. Sensing the same *Hav Murugan* told them " A good drill is nothing but a cumulation of small good individual actions. The whole drill that you do is a total of the individual parts like hand swing, posture etc". The drill instructor had given them yet another life philosophy. While there might be bestselling books on *Atomic habits and Kaizen,* the not so well read, army NCO had told the same philosophy in a manner that was relevant in the immediate context.

The whistle by the seniormost NCO of the camp signalling the end of drill class must have come as a desperate relief for the best cadets bearing the brunt of the sun throwing stinging arrows from its high perch. The moment they were dismissed by Hav Murugan, after getting permission from Menon, the cadets dashed towards the shade of the nearby building and the water camper which was kept there. One cadet fell down, possibly due to the effect of heat and was being attended to by the medical team in the camp. The uniform of all the cadets had huge patches formed by their sweat. Menon noted that he needs to ask the camp commandant, Col Murugan to provide these cadets with lime juice or glucose to avoid dehydration.

After the drill session, now it was their turn to study the service subject. Menon was not sure if he would get adequate attention from the cadets as most of them were dripping wet with sweat. The cadets seemed to be unmindful of it and looked more relieved for being in the shade and under a fan. Menon had fixed his objective to provide conceptual clarity to the cadets in the camp that was currently going on and hence at times, even went beyond the syllabus to ensure a comprehensive understanding of various topics. It being the first day he had been deliberate in choosing the topic as well as in the explanation of the same. He tried to compliment his teaching with some real-life anecdotes from his service life experience.

In between the classes, Menon also kept observing the behaviour and actions of the cadets during the class. Having been a personality assessor, he knew that there was a basic personality set in every individual which was consistent and actions in any occasion didn't deviate much from this basic set. The more spontaneous the action, the more likely it was closer to the basic set. Actions are most spontaneous when one is alone and not under any supervision. But even under conditions of supervision, the actions deviated from the basic set to a small extent only. It was this principle that was responsible for the phenomenon of "How you do anything is how you do everything". He was glad to see both Rashi and Mahesh taking notes, and not being much bothered about the sweat, like a few of the other cadets. Since he was dictating a slightly long answer, he decided to take a walk along the rows of chairs where the cadets were sitting. He found that Rashi had very good handwriting and was taking notes in a supremely organised manner. Mahesh, too had skilfully taken the notes.

As he moved he saw that Saraswathy too was engrossed in taking notes. But as he got closer to her chair, he found that she was trying to hide the notes with one hand and struggling to write them with the other. Though he was behind her chair, her shifting of hand to hide her notes indicated that she must have sensed him coming closer to her. Since she couldn't hide it completely, Menon could make out that she was taking down the notes in *Tamil.* "So, that's what she was trying to hide", a mix of amusement and sympathy went through his mind. He was happy that his objective was being met. He wanted the cadets to become conscious of both their strengths and weaknesses. He decided that he was going to enhance the discomfort in her to such an extent that she would be forced to take action for change. A person will not try to change until he/ she is forced into situations where not changing is more uncomfortable than the discomfort of the status quo. Menon wanted Saraswathy to get extremely uncomfortable with her lack of proficiency in the English language and he made a plan for that, unaware of which Saraswathy continued to take notes believing that she had succeeded in hiding her shortcomings.

After the service subject classes, the cadets reported at the firing range for their firing practice. Col Pathak was the officer in charge of the conduct of firing practice. He was a no-nonsense officer. His philosophy was at complete variance from that of Menon. While doing his initial address to the cadets where he also gave them the safety instructions he made his philosophy very clear. " I am here to provide you with a safe environment to carry out firing, I am not here to motivate you or to push you. So do not expect words of encouragement. You all are preparing for a competition and there will be no one to give these kinds of motivational words during the competition. The ammunition is limited and costly. So do not ask for chances beyond your authorisation. Ensure that the rounds that you get to fire are sent to the target by you, I am in no way responsible for that. Lastly, any violation of the laid down procedure or any deviation from safety norms will make you eligible to be expelled from *MY RANGE*". With the emphasis on the last two words, he made the ownership very clear and also conveyed that they were here as temporary guests and were strictly required to follow the rules. His initial briefing, before commencing the firing, had the desired effect as in the entire duration of the camp, there was neither a single mishap nor was there any requirement to expel any of the cadets. By the tone of his voice and the straightforward manner, Col Pathak had left no doubts in the minds of the cadets that there were going to be no second chances.

Menon keenly observed the actions of the cadets during the firing practice. He was as much interested in the manner in which they carried out their firing as he was in the results. For the cadets, the firing results mattered quite a lot on their chances of getting selected for the team. The maximum marks allotted to firing was one hundred and fifty and a cadet scoring good points gets the definite edge over others. He observed Mahesh and Aswini closely since he had more or less made up his mind about fielding them for the competition.

Firing by NCC cadets is done using a.22 calibre rifle. These rifles are of three types and among them the *sporting rifle* is preferred due to its light weight. As compared to a 5.56mm INSAS rifle or any 7.65mm Caliber weapons, the weapons used by the NCC are of much lesser Caliber. On the command of "cadets lying position" by the range NCO, six cadets who were part of the firing detail took the position at the firing end. As the cadets adjusted their position it was interesting to observe the actions of the cadets. A cadet was displaying nervousness and excitement at holding the rifle, and then there was another who was lying with complete indifference. He found *Mahesh* to be restless with the position. He was clearing the ground in the place where he was lying down. Possibly, the gravel in the place was making him uncomfortable. He was also trying to straighten the groundsheet in the place where he was to take position. He then took the bullets and started rubbing the base of each one of them on the ground sheet. This was generally done to ensure that the rounds don't misfire which is a common occurrence in.22 ammunition. Before the commencement of firing, *Mahesh* was seen conversing with the NCO for a specific rifle which was given to another cadet and the NCO had turned down the request. "Is he trying to build a case wherein he can blame the external circumstances for any possible poor performance in firing? since it was the first practice there was no way for the cadets to know how their performance would turn out to be. Was he preparing for a possible failure and also attributing causes for it to avoid taking the blame for it? Or was he just ensuring that everything was in place to enable a good firing performance? Was it a defensive action in anticipation of the outcome or was it his urge for perfection?", Menon decided to wait for more data before he could come to a firm conclusion, but the restlessness that *Mahesh* was showing, was becoming a matter of concern for Menon.

He also observed *Rashi*. She was lying down with utmost ease. She had adjusted the weapon on her shoulder and was aiming through the sights of the rifle to the target. The entire demeanour was calm and peaceful. She had arranged the five rounds given to her, in a neat line on her right. "Was there no gravel in the place where she was lying? Doesn't the ground sheet have any wrinkles that are disturbing her?, Did she get the rifle of her choice?", Menon wondered. More often our external conditions and experiences are a consequence of our internal state of being. The way we perceive things on the exterior depends on the state that we are inside. Why else would two people sitting on the balcony of the same house perceive the rains differently? One sees the slush forming by the puddle of water on the muddy path and the other sees the amazing rainbow rising in the sky. What one focuses upon does so because of the habit, either we focus on the deficiency or we focus on abundance. It's always a choice.

"Detail Load", the loud command of the NCO got Menon's attention back. "On your target, in your own time, five rounds fire", the NCO continued to blare the orders. Unlike the self-loading rifles, in .22 rifle the round has to be inserted into the chamber using one's hands. With both the round and the chamber being of small calibre, inserting the round at times becomes slightly tricky. A lack of focus and any accompanying anxiety makes it almost impossible to carry out the loading, and quite frequently the round falls down the magazine well i.e. the slot where the magazine is fitted. Menon could see, the hands of certain cadets trembling as they tried to insert the round into the camber. It could be excitement or anxiousness. Surprisingly both have the same symptoms. This aspect can be used to fool your mind into believing that the emotions and feelings one is going through are on account of being excited about an event, which is a positive emotion, rather than being anxious, which is a negative one.

Life is all about keeping the mind in control. At times one needs to fool it to believe certain things the way you want it to believe. It works this way: First, you feed the mind with the thoughts oriented towards the desired objective and then the mind fuels you with the required drive to take action to achieve the objective. Interestingly, these very truths have been stated in so many ways from time immemorial. The Bible says "As you sow, so shall you reap", sow good thoughts and reap favourable results. The same has been expressed by a motivational speaker who said " First you create your beliefs and then your beliefs create you".

"Bang", the first round was fired by one of the cadets. Then there were a series of shots fired one after another. Menon focussed his attention back to *Mahesh* and *Rashi*. Various expressions flashed across Mahesh's face. He grimaced when a round by his judgement may not have gone as planned and then there was a sigh when it did. *Rashi* displayed no expression. Both had their specific type of energy. One was driven more by passion and emotion while the other was dominated by acceptance and tolerance. *Rashi* was a devout believer, but never displayed it in any conspicuous manner, while *Mahesh* was unrestrained about his beliefs. Handling the two personalities would not be possible with the same template. One required constant monitoring and pushing while the other only a gentle nudge. Any interchange of methodology would be detrimental to both of them.

"Unload", the NCO shouted, when he found that all cadet had finished firing their five rounds. After ensuring that the chambers of all the rifles were empty and ensuring that the empty cartridges were accounted for, the cadets were asked to double up to the range butt to get their respective targets. Leading the detail on their way back to the firing point to show the target to Col Pathak and to get their respective scores, *Rashi,* her face beaming with a big smile, and behind her were *Mahesh* and others. *Mahesh* looked disappointed with his performance. " 3 cms grouping size", Col Pathak announced as he measured the spread of the bullets on the target paper. He then proceeded to explain to her the measures that she must adopt to improve her firing performance. "I will improve my performance, sir, she said, retaining the smile on her face. She then proceeded to the place where the cadets were being made to do strengthening exercises. Col Pathak placed greater emphasis on these exercises since he believed that firing is improved off the range than on the range. "The awareness that you can create about your strengths and weaknesses in firing can be best made when you do dry practice. That's the time when you can be fully conscious of all your actions", he told the cadets almost daily.

" 3 cms grouping size", Col Pathak announced again as he checked the target sheet of Mahesh. The group size was the same as that of *Rashi,* but his disposition was in stark contrast to the one displayed by *Rashi.* It was yet another instance of the fact that external circumstances or outcomes are not the deciding factor for the inner state of mind or one's disposition. Apprehensions and aspirations for the future coupled with limiting thoughts and experiences from the past must be the factors that must be responsible for the differing behaviour of the two cadets, Menon mused. Menon by now was sure that he needed to handle these two cadets in unique manners compatible with their distinctive personality.

Menon noticed that there were a few cadets who were able to fire much better than the earlier two cadets. It was important to have cadets of various skills and talents in the group in which the cadets who are intended to be finally inducted into the best cadet event are part. The Group Commander had instructed not to keep too many cadets as reserve for an event, but Menon had been able to convince him to keep the numbers that he wanted. Menon was pleased with himself for keeping the group broad and talking his way out with the superior officer as these cadets who were excellent in specific fields were forcing others to stretch their limits by their performance. Unaware of these factors, *Rashi* and *Mahesh* would at the end of the journey realise the crucial role played by these cadets in the accomplishment of their desires. The minor changes suggested by these cadets in their firing stance, the tips on focussing on the foresight tip, the placing of the elbow in a particular manner, all these seemingly small changes would have an impact on the performance of all the cadets who were part of the Best Cadet event. A few of them who would not be on the final list for the Best Cadet event would later go on to be part of the firing team and win the highest possible awards in it, proving yet again that what we become while trying to achieve something is more important than the achievement itself.

Since it was nearing lunchtime, Col Pathak announced the conclusion of firing practice for the day. After ensuring the correctness of the arms and ammunition the cadets and the staff were dispersed. Menon and Col Pathak walked towards the dining hall for the much-awaited lunch break. "Good cadets, but they won't stand a chance against the cadets from Chennai and Coimbatore", Col Pathak Said. "Coimbatore has the best weapons and also a fantastic range, their cadets have always done well", Col Pathak echoed the opinions that Menon was getting tired of hearing. "I don't accept", Menon muttered under his breath, while just giving a smile which ended the conversation on that topic. Menon could imagine the monk from Myanmar giving him a nod approving his action. Col Pathak must have been wondering about the prolonged smile on the face of Menon, but before the expression was translated to a verbal query, they were greeted by other officers standing at the entrance of the officer's mess. The lunch was finished without much conversation as everyone was looking for the afternoon nap so that they could get recharged for the second half of the day.

The post-lunch session was on current affairs and general knowledge and was conducted by Lt Hemalakshmi, the Associate NCC Officer. The first day was quite disappointing for her since not only were the cadets quite low in their general awareness, but they had not yet come to terms with the hectic camp routine. She found most of them snoozing in the class. Since she was not a person who would give up, nor was she one who would get frustrated with external situations or by the behaviour of others, she immediately found a way to make productive use of the time. She made the class sit in a circle and put a question to the class on how best can they learn general knowledge. Now that the cadets were part of the decision-making, there was significant participation by them in the discussion. The name of a website came up which provided month-wise current affairs which were of immense utility in Best Cadet event preparation since the syllabus for general knowledge assessment included the current affairs of the previous year. Lt Hemalakshmi divided the group of cadets into subgroups and each subgroup was told to prepare a particular sub-section for the first month i.e. January. The different sub-sections were on political situation, economy, who's who, general science and technology and miscellaneous topics. These topics were to be covered both at national and international relevance. By the time the class ended and Menon, strolled into the classroom, Lt Hemalakshmi had been able to make a neat nominal roll showing the division of responsibility and a schedule for covering the General Knowledge syllabus by the end of the camp.

The class soon ended and after the cadets were dismissed for the evening tea, Menon got a briefing from Lt Hemalakshmi on the class and the related activities. Menon was impressed with the way the ANO had tackled the situation and converted what would have been a wasted afternoon into one which set the tone for comprehensive coverage of the topics in days to come by the active involvement of the cadets themselves. The ANO had proved the efficacy of adopting the philosophy of " It may not be your fault, but it is still your problem". By accepting ownership of the problem, she had acknowledged her responsibility for the same and hence retained her "ability to respond". After complimenting her for her innovative and responsible approach Menon walked out of the hall to face the evening sun.

While the sunrise symbolises the time for fresh hope and ideas, the evenings are a time for quiet contemplation. And during today's sunset, he had the philosophy of 'responsibility' that he had just witnessed to contemplate upon. Such thoughtful pondering helps the ideas to be internalized by the mind more effectively. He reflected on how the ANO tackled the situation and how important it was to acknowledge one's responsibility for the problems that one was facing. It wasn't about feeling guilty but about feeling responsible. The feeling of guilt is from an emotional point of view, where you undergo the negative emotions of feeling low and wretched for a certain situation or outcome and blame yourself for the same. On the other hand, feeling responsible is not just a positive philosophy but it also helps the person to retain power and control over the situation with himself. When we blame others for a situation or a particular outcome we also let go of the power we have over the situation and that leads us to face the most hopeless feeling of helplessness or even worse, that of dependency.

After the tea break, the cadets filled the classroom once again for the training session on the next sub-event. Having been in the personality assessment field for almost a decade, this was Menon's area of expertise and passion. As part of the "Best Cadet" competition, a significant portion of marks was given to the aspect of "IQ and Personality". It wasn't just the assessment part that interested him, but the possibility of engineering a person's inner self to a desirable type that had pulled his interest towards it. While most of the psychological theories harped upon the permanency of personality as something which functions within a tight boundary and was, therefore, the destiny of a person, Menon believed that it was possible to bring outright changes in one's personality. Having been a behavioural domain personality assessor, he had been following *Gordon Alport,* the psychologist from the *Gestalt* school of thought. Menon found the definition given by *Alport* to be one which gives hope for making possible changes in an individual's personality. Menon had focussed on that part of the definition which stated the personality to be a dynamic organisation of psychophysical systems within an individual. This was interpreted by Menon, unlike what was propounded by other schools, as personality being an aspect which need not be static and can be changed. And to change, one needs to focus on both the psychological systems and the physical aspects.

This meant that if a person can be made aware of his thoughts, emotions and feelings, which govern his reaction to a stimulus, and then provided with tools and guidance to change those aspects, it can result in a change in the personality. The fact that personality also depends on the physical component i.e. the physical aspects of a person like his health conditions, then naturally leads to the interpretation that if one can follow a routine which keeps one physically fit, it can enable a change in one's behaviour and hence the personality. Menon added support to his hypothesis from the fact that when one completes an exercise routine one feels more energetic, enthusiastic and happy and on the other hand when one is under the weather finds himself to be dull and withdrawn. There exists no doubt that the fitness level of any individual also affects to a great extent his functionality and disposition. It was while he was building his faith in this hypothesis that he came across an incident that was narrated in a book written by a famous motivational speaker. It was of a young boy, who was loving, friendly and a very jovial person. However, he suddenly started displaying violent behaviour, to the extent that he had to be kept away from other children for their safety. His parents thought it to be the changes associated with the difficult stage of adolescence and took the child to a psychiatrist. Fortunately for them, the psychiatrist took an MRI of the brain before prescribing medicines and found that there was a tumour growing in his brain which was pressing against a specific portion of the brain and that is what had led to a change in the behaviour pattern. The tumour was removed and the child was back to the original, loving boy that he was. Even when a person suffers from a minor headache or fever, one finds the person to be despondent, irritable and unenthusiastic. The same person shows a drastically different behaviour when he recovers.

Another factor that weighed in favour of his belief towards personality changes was the fact which has been established through various studies, that most of us during our lifetime utilise not more than 20% of our potential. This meant that even within a fixed basic set of personalities there exists a range of our capacity which in turn means that there exists sufficient scope for bringing changes in oneself. All these aspects had cemented Menon's belief that personality being dynamic, can be changed to a significant degree. Certain changes to the brain circuitry brought about by feeding thoughts of a different kind than the ones that it is used to in the present state coupled with measures to control and channelise emotions can lead to changes in personality. Physical fitness plays its role in controlling the emotions and the concept of self and hence the emotions and feelings that one goes through. Such changes aren't easy, but neither is it impossible. Menon was excited to apply his beliefs once again to the cadets that he was being assigned to train. He was excited because of the two missions that he had embarked upon, one a long-term goal and the second one of short-term significance. The long-term one was his quest towards the larger purpose of facilitating the engineering of young aspirational minds towards the achievement of their maximum possible potential and the short-term one was the objective of making the underdogs achieve, in the forthcoming competition, what was so far thought to be a near impossibility. In his excitement, he hadn't realised that during his quest he would be fighting the fixed and convoluted mindsets of his peers and superiors which would bring to the surface his sense of insecurities and self-doubts and would require all his will and patience to continue to tread on the chosen path without getting detracted or discouraged.

Chapter 5

Sweat, Struggles and Simmerings

Unravelling the Twists and Knots of the Past

As the days of training passed, Rashi and Mahesh continued to display a marked improvement in their performance. It wasn't an easy, smooth journey. While Menon had to deal with the constant negative feedback and pessimistic prediction by his fellow officers on the outcome of the competition, the cadets too had their own set of conflicts to deal with. Mahesh had to deal with the comparison that his father constantly carried out at home. His father was a recently retired army veteran. Though he was not in the officer cadre, he had risen to the highest level possible in his cadre. And even though he had crossed the age of fifty, had maintained himself quite well. He constantly nagged Mahesh, by comparing his routine with that of himself. Coupled with this was the fact that Mahesh had been quite confused while selecting the subject to pursue after completing his school days. Initially, he had opted for Engineering, but within a few months had given up on it to switch to pursuing a Bachelor of Arts in one of the degree colleges in *Madurai.* He also had adjustment issues in his college where his values of standing up for his dignity and more importantly the dignity of his country had brought him into conflict with a few of his professors who had occasionally been involved in verbal diatribe against the nation while conducting routine classes. While other students kept quiet, Mahesh would often take cudgels against the vitriolic opinions against the country by his professor. His refusal to toe the line in the classroom or at least remain a passive listener had filled his professor with a vendetta against Mahesh which the professor took out on various matters related to both academic and non-academic aspects. The other area where Mahesh had decided to stand for his values and had entered into conflict was his refusal to take manhandling by his seniors in NCC. While he understood the importance of discipline and the necessity of punishments at times to enforce the same among the junior cadets, he could never come to terms with the idea of manhandling or hurling profanities. He had got into a scuffle with a senior NCC cadet on this matter and was therefore made a pariah in the NCC company at his college. While his predicament could be attributed to some extent to his lack of sufficient tact and social intelligence, to a considerable extent it was due to his nonconformity with the opinions that stood against his values. Mahesh was looking for validation for his stand and values. During this journey, his obstinacy towards not compromising his values was soon going to be rewarded. Of course, he didn't know it then. He didn't know it when he had empathised with an officer walking under the hot sun at *Idiyappaty* and had volunteered to bring him a glass of water. He didn't know that his pent-up anger and frustration, his untamed energy was soon going to be channelised towards fructifying life-changing achievements.

Rashi too had her devils to fight with. Having lost her father at a very young age, life had turned out to be a formidable challenge for her and her family. The family was running a small church in their village and survived on meagre means. Rashi had a good voice and had decided to use this gift to help augment her family's income. She had joined a small choir group and used to accompany the group to perform in marriages and such functions. The remuneration from these events was quite low and *Marthandam,* being a small town Rashi was forced to travel to far-off places to look for opportunities where she could perform, which involved a lot of time spent in travel. Moreover, most of these musical performances were organised at night and young Rashi would be half asleep by the time she reached back home. She had to gather all her will to get up the next day to go to school. It was during one of these journeys at night that her life had turned topsy turvy. She was seated next to a male member of her choir. Being tired she was in deep slumber during the journey and suddenly woke up to find the person's hand all over her. That must have been going on for quite some time because she found that her dress was dishevelled at places. She froze with fear and shame. " Did he take her lack of resistance that she didn't display for so long as her consent"? " Why did she sleep like a log", was it not her responsibility to be careful"? "What will people say if they come to know that she was molested and what will happen to her family if this meagre income dries up?". She allowed herself to get violated, the only response was the tears that were flowing down her cheeks and the occasional cringing that she did out of revulsion of what she was going through. She thought she would throw up, but she resisted. Any commotion now would wake up others and she won't even get sufficient time to put her clothes in order. Any accidental noticing of the happening without her calling attention to it would only establish her connivance. The man stopped after he either got bored or his hands started hurting. Rashi used the opportunity to immediately put back the clothes in place and cowered in her place folding her hands around her in a protective wrap. She could sense that the man next to him was staring at her possibly with the feeling of power and dominance. She kept her eyes glued to the floor of the bus. As she was getting down at her stop, she took a glance at him and her fear increased when she saw an evil grin playing on his face.

She stumbled like a zombie towards her home. Back home, in the solitary confinement of her room, she broke into inconsolable tears which slowly gave way to shame, guilt and regret. She blamed herself for being not careful and irresponsible, she took the blame for not responding in time and now in hindsight for not responding even after she became aware of the act. She was engulfed by a deep sense of dislike for herself. She often wondered as to why she didn't shout to stop the assault that was being done on her. She detested her voice for failing her. She started doubting and distrusting her sound. From that day on she kept searching for answers. She was looking for salvation from the uninvited deluge of negative chatter that filled her brain. She wanted to find a way out of it but was not sure how to find it. But at her age, she was unaware of the mysterious ways the universe works.

Her search was soon going to end with her being able to rediscover her lost self. She was soon going to redeem herself from the spectre of the past. Of course, she didn't know it then. She didn't know that she was going to get her voice back. She didn't know that the word fear was going to disappear from her lexicon. She didn't know that her tormentor, seeing her grit, determination and success would lower his eyes to be glued to Mother Earth and not raise his eyes again at any 15-year-old girl. She didn't know the fear that would creep into her molester and how he would live the rest of his life in fear of her. The fear of the strength that he would see in the eyes of the girl whose pictures were being flashed on national TV and the print media. She didn't know it then, but the stars and the planets were aligning. The universe was conspiring to lift the young girl to the place where she belonged. But she wouldn't know about it then.

Menon was not aware of the experiences that these two cadets had gone through in their lives so far. But he was aware of their shortcomings. He could gauge it from their behaviour, from their body language, from the hesitancy and the eye movements, from the tone and volume of their voice. He had wondered why *Rashi* who proved to be the most logical among all the cadets during the discussion carried out during the selection process, took so much time to volunteer to come on the stage. He had wondered why *Rashi* would speak in a volume which was nothing short of being just a whisper. He had noticed from far, *Mahesh* getting into arguments with other cadets and staff, and he had noticed the tendency of *Mahesh* to get offended by the slightest of any critical remarks against him. He had watched with concern the tendency of *Mahesh* to sulk when faced with setbacks or failures. He had observed how *Mahesh* after every class/ session came to him to ask for feedback on his performance and to see validation of his every action.

Healing Traumas of the Past

Menon knew that he would have to work through these shortcomings of the cadets to help them shatter the chains of past experiences, which were responsible for the behaviour that they were currently displaying. After a period of time, and time was a commodity that was at a premium, he would have to enable them to create a new perception of themselves. His first task will be to make them craft a brand-new self-image. The two cadets with their completely varied experiences and also the nature of the self-image they carried entailed a completely different approach to handle and mould them to be ready to face the daunting but glorious task in front of them. *Mahesh* needed constant appreciation and validation for his actions and performance. While *Menon* did that for the initial few days, he simultaneously encouraged *Mahesh* to develop self-validation. He changed the words that *Mahesh* used to say about himself during routine conversations, for *Menon* knew that words that one speaks to self is one of the factors responsible for crafting one's self-image. Over a period of time, the vocabulary of *Mahesh* started changing. For instance "Sir, why am I unable to remember what I study for the service subject exam?" Became "Sir, what should I do to enhance my memory of what I study for the exam?" *Menon* also checked him whenever he passed any sarcastic remarks on other cadets. He also encouraged *Mahesh* to be more inclusive in his thoughts. On the other hand, he treated *Rashi* with affection and care. While *Menon* then was unaware of the miseries that this young girl had gone through, except the fact that the girl had lost her father at a very young age, the assessor's mind had the inkling of something amiss in the girl who displayed such low confidence and self-assurance despite being intelligent, logical and above all a person who had excelled both in the field of sports and academics.

While he wasn't aware of the trauma, he was definite that some past experience of hers had a deep-seated impact on this cadet which needed healing. Healing needs love, care, empathy and above all the individual needs a strong sense of purpose that can make the traumatic memories fade away and replace them with meaningful moments.

The Phase I Competition

Finally, the day arrived when everything was going to be put to the test. Not just the level of preparation or skills and abilities of the cadets but also the training methodology of *Menon*. It was also going to test the extent to which *Rashi* and *Mahesh* had been able to resist the influence of their past experiences and their ability to craft a fresh self-image of themselves. Unknown to many, the long-held opinion that only cadets from well-known colleges can meet the criteria of "best cadets" was also going to be tested, the long-held belief amongst the cadets and staff of the directorate that circumstances and situations were a dominant factor in success in these competitions was also going to be tested and the myth was going to be debunked. It is surprising that despite numerous examples we tend to place our beliefs on ideas that put responsibility for an outcome on external sources. While these beliefs get invalidated time and again yet we humans forget these instances and harp on the importance of external circumstances. "What could be the reason for that?" Menon wondered and immediately got the reason too. The examples contradicting routine beliefs are of those who are extraordinary, and for the average, hiding behind external circumstances is a good way to protect their ego. So it is in the interest of the average person to rebuild the belief every time it gets shattered by a trailblazing act. Both *Rashi* and *Mahesh* were going to be tested if they had developed enough strength to break the shackles of the past holding them back and make a choice between remaining amongst the average or joining the league of extraordinary. And that is a choice not just with *Rashi* and *Mahesh,* but with each one of us. Either to let our ego keep justifying our failures and keep us at the same place or to look at our shortcomings straight in the eyes and decide to move out of the comfort zone. To embark on a new journey doesn't require courage alone, but what it requires more is denying your old self the control over the trajectory of your life.

The cadets from other groups had started arriving at the venue for the competition. There were cadets from some of the prestigious institutions of Chennai, Trichy and Coimbatore. *Menon* was responsible for the conduct of the 'Best Cadet' competition and therefore he got busy with the coordination aspects. He lined up the cadets from all the groups to take a head count and check their eligibility for the competition. He took the opportunity to get into casual conversation to understand their level of preparation. " I think my cadets are better prepared than them. They are going to make these overconfident, overestimated and conceited buggers bite the dust", *Menon,* even before he could complete this thought process in his mind, felt sick in his stomach and felt pathetic for his slyness and for 'othering' the cadets from other groups. "Shouldn't all cadets be the same for an officer? Should he not keep the larger picture in mind instead of focusing on short-sighted and parochial objectives? " But if my methodology proves correct then I can apply it on a larger section of cadets and contribute positively towards the larger objective?". "That's right but if the methodology is a viable one, then why have apprehensions about other's preparation?". *Menon* debated with himself in those few nanoseconds and then he gushed " All the best to everyone, let the best person win the competition. Remember it's not the outcome but what you become while trying to achieve the outcome that's more important. You may win or lose in this competition, but make sure that each one of you grows during the competition so that at the end of these ten days you are a changed person" and then he gave a pause for effect, "Physically, mentally and spiritually". As he ended the conversation, he found the cadets from the other group looking up to him without the barrier of 'otherness'. He walked out of the place feeling better about himself and not letting the competition germinate the seeds of meanness and pettiness in him. He genuinely wished the best for all cadets and vowed to himself to consider the outcome of the competition merely as an experience to learn from and not get unduly affected by it irrespective of whether it was favourable or otherwise. He felt more positive about the forthcoming days of competition. When the body and mind is devoid of negative charges, it ought to feel better.

As the officers from the NCC Directorate at Chennai alighted from the taxi at *Idiyapatti,* the first person on whom *Menon's* attention went was the Training Colonel. His gait and the manner of setting aside others' points of view as if they were of little value didn't appeal to *Menon.* In fact, for *Menon,* everything about the Training Colonel seemed outlandish. He was mercurial with unpredictable mood upheavals and to top it all had an insolent tone in his voice even when discussing a mundane topic like weather. *Menon* tried cognitive reframing of his perception of the behaviour displayed by the Training Colonel to not get unduly affected by it. "What vicissitudes of life has he undergone that has made him so caustic in his interactions?" *Menon* thought. "Like they say hurt people hurt people", *Menon* tried to view the behaviour with an enhanced dose of empathy. But despite his efforts, it was difficult to temper the impact of the behaviour of the Training Colonel.

The competition progressed and the performance of the cadets of his group was going exactly as *Menon* had expected and they were living up to the efforts that were put on them by their instructors in various events. As the cadets of his group completed the various steps of the drill test and they performed to a tee, a faint smile crossed the face of both *Menon* and *Murugan*. They exchanged a fleeting glance at each other failing to hide the glee at the fructification of their labour. The satisfaction of witnessing the results of their hard work was worth every drop of sweat that was spilt on the drill ground. The success tasted sweeter as it was achieved in the face of the least expectation and pessimistic opinions on the capability of the cadets of the group to put up even a reasonably good performance. *Rashi* and *Mahesh* knew that they had done well. While they stood ramrod straight on the drill ground and were forbidden to bring any kind of expression on their face, something about them made it evident their realisation of having put up an excellent performance. Humans must also be having an extra sensory perception which can identify the waves generated by emotions that one goes through. *Col Murugan* must have sensed it too for he gave a nod looking at *Menon* which conveyed a mixed feeling of appreciation and surprise.

Excellence and greatness are always accompanied by struggles, setbacks and challenges. It's not that they are mere companions. They in fact in a cyclic roles of cause and effect, are responsible for the creation of one another and also the final outcome of this cycle. If one chooses to get on a path of greatness then he must be prepared for the struggles and when one perseveres through the struggle, excellence gets crafted. To expect greatness without challenges is wishfulness and to look at challenges without being able to see the greatness that lies ahead is pessimism and shortsightedness. And since *Menon's* cadets had been on a roll since the commencement of the competition and were on the path to success, *Menon* was wondering where the companions of excellence were. And within a few hours of him thinking about it, the challenge appeared. Did he manifest it by saying it in his thoughts or was it an obvious thing to occur? *Menon* would never know. But he was going to remember for a long time the moments he was on the edge and the nervous times that he and the cadets would spend worrying about the consequence of the challenge that had come his way. Little did he know that the challenge was going to create conditions wherein he would have to gather all the courage and his inner resources to stand up to his convictions. This in turn would lead him to have greater faith in his convictions due to the favourable results that he would achieve for moving undeterred on his chosen path even in the face of cynicism and ego-centric indignation of others.

And the moment of challenge arrived in the firing range. Both *Rashi* and *Mahesh* did extremely well in the firing. *Rashi* scored the maximum points allotted for the event and had a equanimous joyfulness radiating from her face. *Mahesh* too was close enough though slightly behind the cadets from a group which was designated as the nodal group for training cadets of the entire directorate on competitive firing. *Menon* noticed that while *Rashi* before, during and after firing had retained her calm demeanour, *Mahesh* as usual appeared uneasy and apprehensive. "Why is it that the training didn't have a similar impact on both the cadets?" *Menon* wondered. The fact was that the two were fighting different battles within themselves. And everyone fights their battle based on the experiences they have had. The fight is against the opinions that have been holding within about themselves and the way they have been made to feel. And everyone spends each day trying to prove something, either to themselves or to others. The fact was that while *Rashi* was trying to prove her worth to herself, *Mahesh* was trying to prove to others, because he had always been subjected to comparison where he was always made to feel small and less capable. For *Mahesh,* it was always a race against others. *Rashi* was contended with the progress that she was making every day and when compared to her previous self she had come a long way. The results were quite satisfying to her and therefore she displayed much better emotional stability. Ironically because she wasn't bothered about others, she was faring much better than others. On the other hand, *Mahesh* was always comparing his performance with others. A slight dip in his firing performance and he would start wobbling emotionally. What was compounding the problem faced by *Mahesh* was his tendency to focus on his deficiencies or relatively poor performance rather than paying attention to the spheres he was doing much better than others. The fact that his drill was outstanding and his competitors were nowhere near his performance did little to mitigate the emotional upheavals that he was undergoing due to his slightly lower performance in firing.

It is said that negative emotions attract negative realities into our lives. *Mahesh* was going to experience the same where his focus on his deficiencies were going to threaten his dreams. And this happened at the firing range where *Mahesh* was constantly being tensed about his lower performance. After the firing is over, the cadets were required to bring their targets and show them to the jury, of which the training Colonel too was part. The jury would then count the number of bullet hits on the target and award the points to the cadets accordingly. While the showing of the target by *Rashi* took place without any incident, when it was the turn of *Mahesh,* he was more interested in knowing the score of the other cadets than focussing on his own. When the Training Colonel asked him for his target, *Mahesh* was not paying attention and that irked the Colonel who raised his voice to get his attention. The Training Colonel slowly counted the points and wrote them on the target paper as well as the result sheet. He was about to dismiss him when he asked *Mahesh* "Which cap are you wearing?". *Mahesh* was wearing a cap which the NCC cadets normally wear with tracksuits and not with their uniform with which they were required to wear the combat cap. " Sir I had this cap and so I wore it". *Mahesh* blurted out. *Menon* could sense trouble brewing up. The last thing that he wished for was a confrontation with the jury. He waited with bated breath. There were few more exchanges of words between the Training Colonel and *Mahesh* and the conversation only increased the irritation level of the Colonel. "Don't let this joker go to Delhi" The Colonel blared to *Menon,* his annoyance at *Mahesh* was clearly visible in his tone. It wasn't the belligerence of the Training Colonel that troubled the mind of *Menon* as his propensity towards the same was a well-known element of the Colonel's personality. *Menon* was worried about the spillover effect of this emotionally ladened perception of *Mahesh* by the Colonel in the forthcoming tasks. The tasks that were coming up were the ones in which the assessment was loaded more towards subjectivity. He was worried about the tasks of "Group Discussion" and "Personal Interview" where the element of subjectivity is quite high while judging the performance and allotting points. What added to *Menon's* discomfort was the fact, that it was these "subjective " tasks, that carried the maximum weightage while deciding the ranking of cadets in the "Best Cadet" event.

The assessment system for the event had its bit of twisted intricacies. An assessor generally gave marks around the median in the subjective tasks unless there was a wide variation in performance. The chances of vide variation in these subjective tasks of group discussion, interview was less likely since at every level be it at unit, group or even at the national level a cadet who gets fielded for the competition is reasonably good in qualities like confidence, power of expression, logicality etc which impacts the performance of cadets in these tasks. In such cases, the more objective tests like that of firing and written exams took precedence over the subjective tests. However, the tasks where assessment were likely to be subjective were also tasks with more marks since they dealt with personality attributes. The appropriate logic for such allotment of marks was that a Best Cadet was not just supposed to have skills and abilities but also must have good personality attributes. These subjective tasks were also ones where biases, prejudices and likes and dislikes of an assessor could become deciding factors especially if there is not much variation in performance by cadets in the objective tasks.

Since the group discussion was held immediately after the firing in which the fiasco had occurred, what *Menon* feared manifested in reality. Despite a good performance by *Mahesh,* the Colonel tried to make a case projecting *Mahesh's* performance as a mediocre one in comparison to others. In the personal interview too, *Mahesh* was asked tricky questions by the Colonel. Though *Mahesh,* did manage to give reasonably convincing replies, the Colonel only focussed on those aspects of his answers which confirmed the biases that the Colonel had already formed in his mind. That indeed is the condition typical of a state when one is under high emotional turbulence regarding someone or something. The mind in such a state will keep searching for evidence that confirms the biased thoughts that one has developed. It works both in a positive as well towards a negative direction. In a positive direction, when the mind is filled with an emotional urge towards purposeful goals, then one finds that all things related to it appear before one's eyes. The mind then tends to ignore matters and materials irrelevant to that emotional state and manifests everything related to it. When it is said that, everything that you desire already exists, or when it is said that what you are looking for is looking for you, it only amplifies the phenomenon of confirmational bias. The mind simply looks for evidence that furthers the perception that it has already formed. When you attain an emotional state for success then you find opportunities even in setbacks and on the other hand when you are attuned to thoughts of failure you will find obstacles even in favourable circumstances.

The urge that *Mahesh* had developed throughout training and the way he was attuned towards attaining his objectives, the universe was bound to create the right circumstances as per its laws. It could be due to his urge that fortunately for *Mahesh,* the other two assessors did not readily agree with the opinion of the Training Colonel. While he did try to thrust his biased perception on the others, the two officers in a very polite yet firm way gave their favourable opinion on the performance of *Mahesh.* Since the average of the points given by three assessors was to be taken, due to the low marks given by the Training Colonel, *Mahesh* ranked 3rd in the overall merit in the boy's category. On the other hand, *Rashi* faced no such problem and conveniently coveted the first position in her category. Her demeanour, the logical way of putting across her point of view enamoured the judges and was placed way ahead of other cadets. *Rashi* had done well equally in both the objective and the subjective tasks. She had put a huge margin between herself and others, including the cadets from the prestigious colleges of Chennai and Coimbatore.

If these rankings were to be announced, then *Mahesh* would have no chance of going ahead for the national level competition, and not because of his unsuitability but due to the idiosyncrasy of one of the judges. *Menon* realised that he had to somehow stop the announcement of the results. Among the cadets in the boy's category, the cadet who was being ranked first by the judges was acceptable to *Menon* as well, but he was not satisfied with the cadet who was being ranked second over *Mahesh,* since he was quite underconfident and his abilities that took him so far was his firing skills and academic performance alone. *Menon* was convinced that these abilities could be improved in a cadet over the training period allotted for preparing the cadets of the directorate for the "Best cadet" event at the national level, but to improve upon the body bearing, level of confidence, communication skills and more importantly the urge for the top award etc would take much longer. While *Menon,* having been associated with *Mahesh,* did indeed have an obvious bias towards him, he had consistently made himself conscious of the bias he had for *Rashi* and *Mahesh.* Anything that is done with absolute awareness and consciousness can never be wrong. He knew that his bias had a rationale behind it and was not driven by any automatic compulsive feeling from within. It is just like how an impulsive action during a road rage makes one a murderer and on the other hand, a similar action consciously driven by a greater purpose makes a soldier a hero on the battlefield. The action is the same, the split second in which the action is taken is also similar, but the intention and awareness with which the action is taken makes the difference.

"I request the judges not to announce the ranking of the best cadets during the valedictory day of the selection camp". All eyes turned towards the direction where *Menon was* standing. After ensuring that he had everyone's attention, he continued "If the rankings are announced then the selected cadets are assured of their participation in the national camp and this certainty will induce complacency", *Menon* didn't finish there. "Also, those kept as reserve will hardly take any interest in the future camps and will not put in enough effort to stretch the abilities of the main cadets by posing a challenge to them. Overall announcing the results will not serve the long-term interest of the Directorate team". *Menon* stopped and looked for a reaction from the judges. "I think he has a point", one of the judges spoke even before the Training Colonel could react. The third judge seconded the proposal. The Training Colonel glared at *Menon,* which he ignored and kept his attention focused on the other two judges, though he could feel the stinging stare of the Training Colonel in his peripheral vision. *Menon* could feel the pent-up anger inside the Colonel who could not hold it any longer and blurted " Don't send that Joker to Delhi". This time *Menon* met his stare with a return stare for two reasons. One he had safely manoeuvred the situation to ensure that *Mahesh* didn't lose his chance for achievement and redemption due to the whims of a certain individual and second, he felt that he had to display his disapproval of calling a cadet "Joker", especially one who was making all the efforts to create a turning point in his life. One of the officers who had interfered earlier intervened again to break the starring match between the two officers. "*Menon* please ensure that equal opportunity is given to all cadets to prove their mettle and send the best one ahead to represent the directorate". Said the Senior judge seeing the staring match between *Menon* and the Training Colonel. *Menon* was not just relieved but overjoyed that the senior judge in the panel had given him the leeway to make the final decision based on the progress that the cadets showed during the further training. Keeping with the practice of being conscious of the decisions made by him, *Menon,* said to himself that he would use this free hand granted to him in a responsible manner to select the cadets who were most suited to represent the directorate at New Delhi.

It was baffling for many when three Gold medals were awarded in both the categories i.e. the boys and girls. It was a rare occasion where six cadets were on stage and all were given the gold medal. It was strange, but for *Menon,* who believed that what makes us strange is also what makes us great, anything away from the normal was a good omen. As the valedictory day event got over, *Menon,* after a quick dinner hit the bed. He very soon drifted away to deep sleep. He was tired and more than that it had been quite a fulfilling day. His cadets had proved that it doesn't matter which place one comes from or in which school or college one gets to study, finally, it is the urge and faith in oneself that determines the attainment of the set objective. *Menon,* at the end of the day, was feeling validated as his philosophies that he had followed quite religiously had borne fruits. He could now, with better confidence use the same philosophy to train the cadets for the prestigious event to be held in the capital.

The Final Selection

While *Menon* had felt elated at the success of his manoeuvre to ensure that *Mahesh* gets his due, he didn't know that the arrangement of not announcing the results for the "Best Cadet" event, had also sown the seeds for a problem that he would face shortly. And this problem had a name, *Shalini*. Shalini was from the prestigious Christian College of Chennai which had traditionally been giving the "Best Cadet" to the directorate team. *Shalini* was an attractive girl who was also an accomplished dancer. Being from an acclaimed college she carried the airs about her. Unknown to *Menon,* this cadet had harboured the thought that none other than her would be finally selected to represent the directorate at Delhi. But the fact was that she was left far behind by *Rashi,* who had emerged as the clear winner and all the judges had voted favourably for her. *Shalini* was retained merely to pose a challenge to *Rashi* so that her abilities are stretched to develop her qualities to meet the challenges and not get into complacency in the absence of a threat to her place in the directorate team.

Unaware of what was precipitating in others' minds, both the mentee and the mentor got headlong into the training regimen. The cadet who was adjudged the best in the boy's category was *Tarun* who was from a lower middle-class family and had his share of struggles. He too, like *Mahesh* was from the small town of *Tenkashi,* the scenic spot on the southwestern border of Tamilnadu with Kerala. He carried the values and beliefs that he had inculcated during his childhood days in this remote town before he shifted to Coimbatore to pursue his degree. He was initially bedazzled by the liberal culture of the metro and faced the conflict between the values that he had grown up with and the one he was witnessing around him. There was peer pressure to have a fit body with protruding abs and there was this compelling requirement to have a female partner if one was to be considered successful in his teenage. *Tarun* initially got carried away by these newly found values that he had to adapt to. But one day he paused to think about the mad race he was getting into and he was reaching nowhere. He was meeting failures and heartbreaks and in the deluge of emotional upheavals, his dream of flying in the sky was getting buried. He was intelligent and sharp, but what made him stand out was his unmatchable perseverance. He also had a great ability to face criticism and yet take it in his stride. And on top of it all, he was a fanatical optimist. He had a vast expanse of energy inside him and he was looking for a mentor to enable him to channel the energy in the desired direction. Another quality that set him aside from others was his total control over his emotions. Except for an occasional smile, *Menon* was intrigued by the lack of display of any kind of emotions by this cadet.

When *Tarun* first met *Menon,* he wasn't expecting much support or warmth from him as he was an officer with another group and in a competition, it was expected that the motivational talks by officers were restricted to their cadets alone. However, he found *Menon* showed no difference in treating the cadets from other groups. The line said by *Menon* that stuck with *Tarun* was that "it's not the goal that matters, but what you become while trying to achieve the goals. Because goals are temporary and they dissipate once achieved, but the changes that you bring within you are permanent and they continue to help you in achieving all the goals in future". And that was indeed an "Aha" moment for *Tarun.* "Maybe the universe put this man in my path to help me get my wings", *Tarun,* who had a childhood dream of joining the Indian Airforce thought. He decided to focus on the journey of TSC and to concentrate on the development that he would make every day in himself rather than merely focusing on the desired end of the TSC journey. *Tarun* was soon going to realise one of the ultimate truths that it is when one focuses on the process rather than the outcome that the likelihood of achieving the desired outcome increases.

Meanwhile, *Mahesh* was struggling with his insecurities and fears. He was apprehensive of the result and what would happen if he didn't get selected for the final team to go to Delhi. While *Tarun* with his all-around good performance had created a niche for himself as most suited as "Best cadet", *Mahesh* had to compete with another cadet to make the grade. While *Mahesh* was excellent in Drill and Personality-based tasks, the other cadet was beating him in firing and academic subjects. And that caused him a lot of anxiety regarding his chances of making it to the directorate team. He was more focused on his deficiencies rather than his strengths. Amongst the three cadets in the boy's category, it was *Mahesh,* who had the best physical bearing. He was tall, athletic and had a chiselled face. He looked like a Bollywood hero. But then the external appearance in no way can compensate for the lack of self-esteem or self-image. Years of facing comparison and criticism had made him oblivious to the positive qualities that he was bestowed with and instead was focused on his weaknesses. For a quality that a boy of his age would have strutted about, *Mahesh,* because of his self-image could not even perceive its presence.

While each cadet was struggling with his/ her insecurities and fears, collectively too they had to face the derision and ridicule from the other staff who were part of the camp. Unlike other events like drill, obstacle training etc, the "Best cadets" were exclusively under the tutelage of an officer. These cadets owing to a larger number of events that they had to participate in, could not come for the central gathering, called "Roll Call" in the armed forces, where all the persons of a unit are required to gather for a head count and to receive the orders for the next day. This lack of control over a section of cadets was resented by the lower-level staff and they lost no opportunity either to award punishments like push-ups, rolling etc on the slightest pretext or to embarrass them in front of other cadets. One such staff was *Subedar Venu,* who looked forward to harassing these cadets for flimsy reasons. The cadets either due to fear of consequences or due to the norms prevailing in NCC of giving respect to the seniors, never reported the matter. The Subedar at times also indulged in manhandling the cadets which also went unreported, until the day when he hurled abuses at *Mahesh.* In the volley of profanities, he had spewed a few involving his parents. *Mahesh* was unable to take it and came straight to *Menon* to report the matter. *Menon* was aghast at the torment, both mental and physical that these cadets had been subjected to. The matter was escalated to higher authorities and the Subedar was relieved of his duties in the camp with immediate effect. *Menon* could not make out the reason for such apathy towards cadets especially when they were here at the camp sacrificing their attendance in the colleges and allocating their time for these camps hoping for a turning point in their lives. "Maybe the need for control and the feeling of having the power overwhelms the human need for empathy and compassion", *Menon* thought.

The removal of the Subedar gave hope to the cadets that their voice would be heard and that there are boundaries beyond which a punishment whether physical or in any other form need not be accepted. It also raised the morale of the "Best cadets", and they were treated better by the staff and were given their due by other cadets as well. With training back on track and with the day of final selection approaching fast the cadets started putting their best. *Menon was* sure about *Tarun and Rashi.* It was *Mahesh who,* despite his capabilities was still not coming up to the mark. His competitor too was not making much improvement in his areas of weakness which were the personality-based tasks like group discussion and interviews. Also, his bearing and overall body language gave away his underconfidence. However, these were subjective factors and the selection had to appear objective and needed to be justified by the points that the cadets were scoring in the various events that were part of the "Best cadet" competition. Going by the points alone, *Mahesh's* competitor seemed to be having a slight edge. *Menon* tried to focus on this cadet hoping that he would improve upon his qualities to build, within himself, a fighting chance at winning at least the silver medal at the national level. However, despite his best efforts the cadet didn't seem to overcome his inhibitions and apprehensions. Despite his good performance in both firing and the written exam on service subjects the cadets always wore an anxious appearance and was found sulking most of the time. It affected his participation in the personality-based tasks which had the maximum points in the Best Cadet event. Both *Mahesh* and this cadet were no match for *Tarun* who had crafted a firm place for himself in the probable contingent. The choice for the second participant in the boy's category was going to be tough for *Menon*.

There are occasions in a man's life when he needs to weigh between what is morally correct and what suits the situation in a practical way. In a last bid to raise the sagging morale of *Mahesh,* hoping that it would make him utilise his potential in a more effective manner free of the stress that he was imposing upon himself, *Menon* did what was out of the rule book. He called *Mahesh* separately and told him that he had made the final decision on the cadets who were to go to Delhi and that *Mahesh* was on the list. Mahesh knew that he was wrong on two accounts. Firstly, he had taken no such decision and therefore had lied to *Mahesh,* hoping that it would ease his stress level and enable him to function on the tasks and display efficiency. *Menon,* was sure that he would have to go as per the numbers reflected on the result sheet and if the other cadet even had the slightest edge in numbers, he was bound by the rules to take him as part of the contingent to Delhi and not *Mahesh.* He realised his second mistake when that evening the other cadet expressed his desire to quit the competition. As the other cadet stood in front of him to announce his decision, *Menon* found it difficult to meet his eyes. "Did *Mahesh* spill the beans and brag about his inclusion in the team?". Apart from losing his moral standing in his own eyes as a mentor, he would also have to face official consequences if the matter escalates. And was his aim to ensure that one of "his" cadets wins the Best Cadet event at the national level so that his mentorship gets validated? What about his philosophy of "It's not the goal that matters but the person you become while you are trying to achieve the goal?". Was he going against his philosophy? The train of thoughts going through his mind was causing a long uncomfortable silence between the two. He had to speak up. "What made you decide to quit?", *Menon* asked. "Sir, I feel I am not making much improvement and I don't see my chances of making it to the team", the cadet said. A stinging sensation went through *Menon*. "Did he make his preference for *Mahesh* too obvious?, he thought. *Menon* was feeling empty, but he gathered himself "Shouldn't you wait for the official announcement of results rather than make negative speculations?". "While winning a race is important, completing it is also no mean feat. If I were in your place I would have waited" *Menon* felt his voice trailing off as he felt the emptiness of his own words. But the next day he learnt that the cadet had decided to stay and complete the journey rather than quit in between.

Not announcing a clear-cut winner during the Inter Group competition had given a chance to *Mahesh* and hence to *Menon* to select the most suitable cadet and also defeat the ego-driven machinations of the Training Colonel. But unknown to *Menon,* this ambiguity was fomenting a new challenge for *Menon. Shalini,* the cadet from one of the prestigious colleges of Chennai had made up in her mind the certainty of her place in the final team. The past reputation of these colleges in sending the best cadets as part of the directorate team coupled with the unassuming nature of *Rashi* must have crystallised her belief in the inevitability of her being the ultimate choice as part of the directorate team. There was no doubt that she too gave her best shot at the event. She didn't merely depend on the reputation of her college instead she did everything within her means to keep up with that reputation. It was a sheer chance that this particular year, *Rashi,* a cadet from a lesser-known town and from a group considered to be the underdog had decided to prove all the long-held concepts and beliefs to be wrong. When the final list of selected candidates was announced, *Shalini* unable to accept the verdict, contested the same vociferously. She called *Menon,* to ask about the perceived injustice done to her. She even gave a written complaint, but since there was a consensus amongst all the judges from the directorate regarding the suitability of *Rashi* over other girl cadets to represent the directorate team at New Delhi, no one took cognisance of the complaint. It did lead *Menon* to introspect about the conduct of training and the methodology adopted for the selection of cadets for such events. In hindsight, *Menon* realised that while he was putting additional pressure on *Rashi* by admonishing her for her little flaws while ignoring the same of others and also when he asked her to imitate some of the good aspects of other cadets, he had not realised the distortion in perception that he was creating in the minds of the other cadets both regarding theirs and Rashi's performance and chances of making it to directorate team. The fact that *Shalini* was not checked much by *Menon,* made her rightly believe that she was performing much better than *Rashi.* But at the same time, he was also amazed at how the self-confirmation bias makes a person overlook the evidence and data that goes against their beliefs and convictions. There was an incident when *Rashi* despite being sick and having gone through bouts of vomiting had still given a wonderful lecturette. The drill ustad always had a word of praise for *Rashi* for the exemplary standards that she displayed which was way beyond the performance of her compatriots. *Shalini* had missed all that and merely focussed on the times *Rashi* was castigated by *Menon.* In certain group discussions even though the time allotted was 20 minutes, *Menon* would terminate the group discussion within 8 to 10 minutes and *Rashi* who was a slow starter in most of the discussion would be rudely surprised because she had the habit of listening to everyone before contributing with very well thought out logical points. *Rashi* would give a surprised look at *Menon* because there would be many discussions where *Rashi* would not have spoken a word and the discussion would have moved to the next topic. "If you wait for too long you are going to miss the bus", *Menon* would say to the group while solely targeting *Rashi.* He wanted *Rashi* to become an early entrant in the discussion as this improvement in her, combined with her inherent trait of being logical, would make her unassailable in any of the personality-related tasks. However other cadets in the group were not aware of *Menon's* intentions towards bettering the quality of initiative of *Rashi* and merely saw her lack of participation in many discussions as her deficiency which would lower her ranking amongst her fellow cadets. Little did they know that with each discussion *Menon* was noting the improvement that *Rashi* was making in terms of time within which she made her entry into the discussion and was reasonably satisfied with the progress.

Shalini, on the other hand, was always an early entrant. Even though many times the points that she contributed towards the topic would be superficial and even irrelevant, it didn't stop her from initiating the discussion. When she saw that in several discussions where she took the initiative and participated consistently, *Rashi* could not even make an entry and the discussion was terminated, it enhanced her belief of being the one who would make it top of the directorate team. In hindsight, *Menon* could not fault *Shalini* for the perception she had developed. *Menon,* made a mental note to ensure the carrying out of perception management of cadets in future so that no cadet visualises any misplaced notion of either himself or others even inadvertently. Amidst the whining, complaints and tears, *Menon* announced the final team. There was bickering and some subtle indirect pillorying, especially from the officers of the group which had traditionally been fielding the Best Cadets for the Directorate at the event in Delhi. The snide remarks were made in the presence of *Menon* in an insidious manner. *Menon* had tried to keep up his demeanour so as not to get unduly affected by these remarks. However, these remarks did make him question himself. "What if I indeed have not done the selection correctly?", "Did I make a mistake by selecting these cadets from the relatively unknown areas?", "What if these cadets crumble under the pressure of having to prove themselves and their performance gets affected by their own opinions and that of the others?" *Menon* was sure that the cadets, like him, also might be being made targets for ridicule and malevolence. Breaking traditions and deviating from the norms always has its side effects. If one doesn't learn to accept it, then one has to be satisfied with the status quo. But being satisfied and maintaining the status quo is not how positive changes have occurred in the world. With these introspections and having got some convincing replies to his queries, *Menon* felt more confident and assured of his decisions.

In the meantime, the teams for the rest of the events too were finalised and the officers got busy with procurement of clothing and other accessories for the cadets who had finally made it to the contingent. *Menon* was pleased to know that *Saraswathy,* had made it to the final list in the Obstacle Course event and would get an opportunity to move out of the small town of *Tirunelveli* and get the exposure of being in the nation's capital and meeting cadets from all over the country. *Menon* hoped that this exposure would broaden her horizon about life and make her dreams bigger.

Now that the training period was over, everyone was looking for validation of the outcome of the event—the cadets about their abilities, physical and mental and the mentors on the quality of their mentorship. *Menon* was looking for validation for his training philosophies as he had the dreams of playing a greater role in future, of assisting individuals to realise their ultimate potential and to craft their personalities to convert their dreams to reality. He aimed to help a maximum number of people break the chains holding them back and move forward with absolute faith in their abilities and potential.

Chapter 6

The End is Always Glorious

Controlling eighty-plus cadets milling around at the Madurai railway station was the worst nightmare for the NCC staff. The problems were compounded by the presence of parents, some of whom were sending their wards for the first time to such a far-off place as the national capital. The background from which many of the cadets had come was of the type where the name Delhi was heard only in the news and each one had made their perception regarding the national capital based on what they had read or heard. The reasons why the capital was in the news were not very pleasant. Road rages, accidents, political strikes, bomb blasts and the one which made the parents of girl cadets cringe with apprehension was the frequent reports of molestation and harassment of girls. *Menon* and other officers had a challenging time explaining to these parents that their children would be safe in the DGNCC complex and that for the entire duration of the camp, they would be under their watchful eyes.

Another thing that *Menon* noticed with amusement, was the mothers feeding their children in the station. Every cadet whose parents had come to the station had his/her mouth stuffed with homemade goodies. It was as if the cadets were going to be on fast for the next 10 to 12 days. *Menon* was worried that such overeating would lead to stomach upsets and affect their performance in the oncoming competition, but he knew that he was helpless in front of the emotionally ladened gestures that these parents were displaying, which even though misplaced was not something he could brush aside. *Menon,* as the time for the departure of the train came closer, was worried that some cadets might resort to boarding the train while it was on the move which could result in some serious accident. The staff had a tough time convincing the parents to let go of their wards to board the train in time.

Amidst this chaos, *Menon* had not missed giving some last-minute advice to his cadets. He reminded *Mahesh,* not to lose his cool and not to be anxious about the outcome and instead focus on the task at hand, *Rashi* to keep her faith in her abilities and *Tarun,* to not think it's over until the last event is done with. As the train moved out of the slumber, working hard against the inertia of having been at rest, *Menon,* kept pace with it, yelling tips and advice and anything that came to his mind until he found his voice choking. He left the window rails when he couldn't stand the lump in his throat any more. His cadets were on their own now. He could do nothing more for them other than keep them in his prayers. The train was carrying bundles of hopes, dreams and ambitions. The outcome of the events had the power to either nourish them and make them blossom or crush them under the weight of not meeting the expectations. *Menon,* waited until he could see the train no more. With the stimulus for his ongoing emotion now having been distanced, the rational part of the brain started gaining control and *Menon* wondered if it was right to have such bouts of emotions. The answer to the question appeared out of the repertoire of knowledge that he had gathered from various books. Emotions are best defined as energy that has been put in motion. It is the vibrations within oneself that get depicted as emotions. And one of the universal truths is that the vibrations within you attract similar vibrations from outside. Energy when it moves creates matter or what is called reality, and hence it is of great significance to be consciously aware of the vibrations that one is experiencing. The universe is neutral when it goes about creating the reality around a person in tune with one's vibrations. It makes no distinction between positive and negative. A person simply attracts people and situations based on the vibrations that one puts across into the universe. This brainwave created an awareness of the vibrations that *Menon* was putting into the universe. He realised that it was up to him on the type of thoughts that he was putting out in the universe. From being apprehensive about the cadets being on their own, he consciously changed it to that of excitement of looking forward to how his mentees would withstand situations on their strength and emerge victorious. This change in thoughts brought a shift in the energy that he was experiencing. From despondency, there was now excitement and optimism. He smiled at the realisation that finally it's the thoughts that one goes through that decide the state one is in. And to change the thoughts was also completely in one's control. It was just a matter of practising it and making it a habit. Little did he know that one of his cadets was going to use this very philosophy, of choosing the vibrations that one experiences, to ensure the achievement of the goals.

The Delhi Duels

As the train slowly came to a halt at the New Delhi railway station, the heartbeat of the cadets increased its pace. A mix of emotions, which could be described in one word as nervous excitement gripped the air. The staff were shouting orders at cadets who were bewildered by the mere fact that they were stepping onto the national capital. Not that the station was in any way different from Chennai or any other city that they were coming from, but the perceptions that they had crafted within themselves made them go through the feelings that they were going through. There lies a paradox in the aspect of emotionality. On one hand, awareness of our emotional state helps us to be objective in our view, and on the other hand, there are instances where it is emotions that drive us towards achievements, innovation and discoveries. An awareness of emotions of excitement makes it disappear which is counterproductive for a person going to participate in a competition. The only way to take advantage of this paradox is to keep our intentions purposeful and in line with the larger good. Emotions backed by the right intentions will always move life on the right track and even when the person is under the sway of the emotions it will only facilitate or even better, boost a person in the accomplishment of their goals.

Menon had trained his cadets to always have the right intention and not to carry within themselves any negative charge like that of jealousy, hatred, anger or any element of unhealthy competition. He constantly made them keep their focus on improving themselves and stretch their limits rather than comparing themselves with others. When *Rashi, Tarun and Mahesh* stepped on the platform at the New Delhi railway station, each one was thinking only of the moment when they would excel in the event for which they had trained. Since they had carried the intention of only focussing on their performance without comparing with others they found equanimity even when the air was filled with the competitive spirit which was at times over the top.

There were cadets of other directorates too who were assembling in the platform for their count-up and thereafter moving to the bus that was waiting to take them to the DGNCC complex. There was a palpable animosity in the air with a few side glances and some conspicuous glares at one another between the cadets of different directorates. Finally, the contingents from various directorates boarded their respective buses and proceeded towards their common destination. As the buses moved it was accompanied by the shrill battle cries of each contingent. The obvious aim was to gain ascendency over others through shouting since that was supposed to be indicative of the confidence that a contingent had in winning the competition and hence of their morale.

As the buses reached the ground at the DGNCC complex they were parked in their respective slots in a well-rehearsed and disciplined manner. Drivers who were the old hand had kept a straight face throughout the journey and were quite detached from all the excitement that was happening behind them. For them, the shouting was as much the part of the drill that they had been used to as was the parking of their vehicles in respective slots. The new ones partook in the excitement and stole a few looks in the rearview mirror to not lose out on all the excitement that was filling up the vehicle. As the cadets started alighting from the vehicle, a few exchanged pleasantries and smiles which was of course frowned upon by the hardcore loyalists from the respective contingents. However, as the ice broke and the cadets started mixing, the air of animosity was replaced with bonhomie and friendly chats. The next few days were going to witness the blossoming of great friendships between cadets of different directorates. *Mahesh* had made acquaintance with a cadet from Tripura and was busy exchanging notes with him. *Tarun* was trying to find out the best cadets from other directorates so that he could gauge their strengths and weaknesses. *Rashi* was standing in the drill ground trying to soak in the ambience and as instructed by her mentor was trying to visualise how she would be marching there on the D day. Despite venturing out of Tamil Nadu for the first time she was feeling quite at home at this place even though the weather, language and culture were quite strange as compared to what she was used to. It was her strong purpose that was the sole reason for the attunement that she was experiencing with this strange place. She felt her firm footing on the drill square where they had gathered for the fall-in before moving to their designated barracks. She felt as if the drill square had already been conquered by her. Was this moment of visualisation, wherein she was absolutely in sync with the place, that was responsible for her achievement or was this feeling and visualisation merely a consequence of the hard training that she had gone through and the mindset change she brought in herself and the strong desire that she had developed towards her gaols, she would never know. But what was going to be etched in her mind forever, would be the feelings and emotions, the vibrations in her body and mind that preceded the achievement of her cherished desires. She will remember the charged-up ambience around her and the constant flow of inexplicably abundant energy within her. In the flow of the emotions within her, she took her right leg up and stamped it hard on the ground. *Tarun,* who was standing close to her looked at her with amusement. He understood the passion with which *Rashi* undertook any task. But as she stamped, she felt an intense pain shooting up from her heels right to her brain. She froze with fear. Has it returned? Will it snatch away her dreams? She fought hard to stop her tears from welling up. *"How will you know that you are on the path to greatness? The universe will put hurdles on your path to test your desire and faith and then you know that you are on the path to greatness".* "That's what Menon sir told us", she tried hard to put a smile back on her face and started regaining the confidence that had started ebbing with the shooting pain. She understood that this was a message from the universe. She was about to achieve what she had never done before. She was going to be a part of the folklore in NCC which will be told for a lot of time to come. She understood the omen. There was history going to be created and she has been chosen to write it as the protagonist in it.

After the count-up and the registration were over, the cadets were shown their barracks. The NCO of the directorate who had come a few days earlier at the venue told them about the distribution of cadets in various rooms and also issued them with mattresses, bedsheets, blankets etc. The cadets had to keep the area clean from day one as the TSC competition also had an event called "Line Area Competition". It was suspected that this competition was made part of the event primarily to ensure that the directorates maintain their lines in a clean and hygienic manner so that cadets don't fall sick as well as to cater for the VIP visits to the area. Some of the directorates took this event too seriously and the cadets slept on the floor one day before the Line Area Competition so that the bed and the surrounding areas don't get disturbed. *Rashi* opened her shoes as soon as she got to her allotted place. She got a sinking feeling when she saw that the skin of her feet had turned red. She knew that it was just a matter of days before it would turn into painful sores with blood oozing out of it almost constantly for some days till it started subsiding. She had been suffering from this affliction since birth and had accepted it as a part of her life. Within the meagre means at her disposal she had tried to seek all kinds of medical treatment from allopathy to local medicants, however to no avail. Sitting on her bed and gazing at the reddishness on her feet, she could only pray that the sores would get delayed till her drill tests got over as that was the event where this ailment could have a major impact on her performance.

The Competitions

The Best cadets of the Madurai group had started their journey as the underdogs. There were not many expectations from them. The cadets in the other events like the Obstacle course competition were expected to do well and shore up the position of the directorate to the top slots. The boy's team was considered to be formidable with cadets constituting from the villages of Tamilnadu and were rugged and naturally well-built due to the physical work that they were required to do in their daily routine. Running behind the cattle, climbing up coconut trees to harvest the crop, swimming in the village ponds, trekking up the hills to fetch firewood etc were the activities that had built their bodies to be strong and supple to tackle obstacles like the balance, double ditch, vaults etc with quite ease. It was a pleasure to watch them fly over these obstacles with such ease that one would be tempted to consider tackling these obstacles to be facile unless one tries to do it themselves. But if brute strength alone mattered then humanity would not have evolved to the state that we are in today and would have merely roamed around the wild like any other species from the animal kingdom. The village lads were awed by the strange surroundings they found themselves to be in. They could only hear cadets speaking in Hindi or English and even the *Ustaads* shouting orders in Hindi which they hardly understood and needed someone to translate to them.

The event started with the obstacle course competition for the boys. The race started well for the directorate team and the boys seemed to be on the verge of creating a record for the minimum time in which any team had completed the course. That's when the disaster struck. When one of the boys was crossing the Zig Zag Balance, the judge manning the obstacle said something in Hindi and the cadet tackling the obstacle thought that he had not done the obstacle correctly and tried to repeat it and the judge tried telling him that there was no objection from his side and the cadets again misinterpreted the conversation. Precious time was lost and since it is the last cadets' time that is counted as the time taken by the directorate, the team finished with one of the worst timings ever. There were protests amongst rumours of conspiracy and intentional misguidance, but the result stayed. Fortunately, the debacle suffered by the boy's team did little to demoralise the girl's team who also like the Best Cadets had started as the underdogs and weren't considered that good as the team consisted of girls who were lean and looked weak. The girls' team finished the course with second second-best timings of the competition. The performance of the girl's team lifted the morale of the contingent. Contrary to the expectations the teams performed moderately in most of the other events. The overall position of the contingent was likely to be disappointing.

The Best Cadet events were kept in the end and unfortunately for *Rashi,* by this time the redness in her feet had turned to sores and they had also broken. On certain evenings when she would come back after attending the camp schedule and drill practice and open her shoes, she would find her socks drenched in blood. While she used to talk to *Menon* every day, she resisted giving any input regarding the suffering that she was going through. The infection became so severe that on the day of the drill competition, she had to be carried to the drill ground

piggyback by other cadets of the contingent. With great difficulty, she had been able to put on her boots. But her pains were overwhelmed by her desire for success as she knew that only an outstanding success in her life could erase the memories that made her spend many a sleepless night. She had considered this journey not as one for merely achieving success but for redeeming herself. The universe had given her this opportunity and she couldn't fail herself. She took her position in the line, determination and grit replacing any traces of pain that she was going through while being carried to the drill ground. Cadets were called one by one by the drill *Ustaad* and on their turn were required to display the complete procedure lasting about ten minutes in front of the panel of judges. The drill *Ustaad* shouted "Next". All the eyes were on *Rashi.* "Cadet Saavdhan", *Rashi* yelled the command for herself hoping it would drown any remnants of pain that her body going through. As she brought down her right foot in one fell swoop after taking it as high as possible and stamped her feet hard on the toughened tarred drill ground, a shock travelled from her heels up to the pain centre in her brain. Her mind and body pleaded with her to stop the madness. "Your body and your mind are not exactly your friends, they are the ones that more often than not come in the way of your success", *Rashi* tried to recollect the words told by her *Menon sir.* Clenching her teeth, she kept her body and mind aside and looked ahead at her goal. She could visualise the gold medal and the applause that she would be receiving from the audience. And then she felt no more pain. Every move, every step with every command was carried out with clockwork precision. It was not as if she was taking the actions in a conscious realm, but out of unconscious memory of the umpteen number of practices that she had done at *Idiyappatti.* When she gave the final salute to the panel of judges, indicating the termination of her drill, there was a spontaneous "Well done", by all three judges from the DGNCC. The drill

Ustaad who was coordinating the activity unknowingly was giving a nod of acknowledgement and appreciation, a very rare gesture from *drill ustad,* who always keep a straight face and don't let the slightest of emotions even have a fleeting appearance on their face. As *Rashi* came into conscious awareness, the pain gushed back with vengeance. She took a few steps and could walk no more. Everyone was surprised as to how a person who was a moment back with tons of energy was now writhing in pain on the drill ground. Her compatriots who were nearby knew it. They rushed to open her shoes, but they wouldn't budge. Ultimately, the shoes had to be ripped open with a knife. The sight that awaited those who had gathered around her made even the strongest of the military hearts present skip a beat. Even her socks that was drenched with blood, could not be taken out. All the sores in her feet had broken and the blood was oozing out at quite a pace due to the brisk physical activity which *Rashi* had gone through that had increased the pressure of blood movement within her. Since there was no point in trying to give her any first aid, she was immediately evacuated to the military hospital. By evening she was back to her barracks with her battered feet covered with layers of bandage but her soul rejuvenated with fresh draught of enthusiasm, hope and joy of giving her best in the most trying circumstances. The rest of the tasks went as smoothly as sliding a hot knife through butter. She was unstoppable in group discussion and every cadet in the group was seen addressing her and seeking validation of their opinion from her. She was the unanimous choice as the defacto leader of the group. Probably, after having witnessed the iron will of *Rashi* at the drill square, the rest of the cadets had accepted the inevitability of the results going in favour of her. By the end of the event, every cadet and staff at the venue of the competition knew her by face and name. She was the obvious choice when the directorate was asked to forward names of cadets for the award of the DGNCC commendation card. The valiant performance of *Rashi* had given her directorate something to cheer about and the flagging morale of the contingent started shoring up.

Tarun and *Mahesh* too had performed very well in the boys category. As expected, *Tarun* had emerged as the clear-cut winner, putting a wide gap in points between him and the runner-up. *Mahesh* was a close third. When the results were declared it was a matter of great pride for the directorate that all the three cadets who had been fielded in the Best Cadet event had won a medal each and the top positions in both the boys and the girl's category were bagged by the cadets from the directorate. While overall the directorate had not done well, the directorate team and staff from the event had learnt important lessons which would facilitate their bouncing back in the competitions in the coming year. This was the time to reflect on the methodology adopted for the preparation and selection of the team. The home ground advantage that the cadets of the group, who were responsible for the conduct of the intra-directorate competition, had was lost in the unfamiliar environs and situations of New Delhi. The directorate had also made the folly of underestimating the other contingents and had gone as per their past experiences and opinions. It was forgotten that the preconceived notional templates of "ruggedness in the villages" and "intellect in the cities" no longer held water. The tendencies in the selection of the team were governed by this philosophy and were contrary to the data available and this proved to be the contingent's undoing. The sparks of brilliance especially by the girl's team in the obstacle course and by the best cadets ensured that the directorate looked forward with hope and belief that all was not lost and that with some refinements much could be achieved in the coming year.

It took some time for the results to settle in both for the winners and for those who couldn't come up to their expectations. The revelry by the winning team soon subsided and the sagging faces of others started looking up. There was an exchange of consolations and congratulations and of course the contact numbers and social media accounts. Emotions and feelings are temporary visitors and should never be given permanent residency by identifying oneself with them. What it translates into is that one should never call himself a winner or loser, instead realise that one is only going through the feeling of winning or losing. And feelings are ephemeral and transient. One moment there is a surge and the next moment they will just disappear if you allow them to. Holding on them either makes you despondent and pessimistic or it makes you complacent. At the same time looking at these events as experience helps one to get inspired, attain hopefulness and also learn lessons to overcome the shortcomings for future endeavours.

Chapter 7

A Destination Inspires a New Journey

Menon had boarded the train from *Chennai* to go to his home town. He had opted for the window seat in the chair car and was fortunate to be allotted one. He always enjoyed the scenic beauty that was arrayed on either side of the track that took the train to God's Own Country. When the train started, he noticed that the two seats next to his was unoccupied. He always liked to strike up conversations with his fellow passengers and was therefore disappointed to find them vacant. Little did he know that the privacy that he had been bestowed with in this journey would enable him to be immersed and soak in completely the joy that he was soon going to experience.

As soon as he had settled down with his book, he received a call from the NCC Group Commander. He was given the news of mixed performance by the contingent and also regarding the exemplary performance of the best cadets. He felt a surge of accomplishment on hearing that the top positions in the best cadet event were bagged by his cadets. It was as if a destination had been reached. And with the destination also comes a feeling of emptiness since the purpose of the past few months had been accomplished and *Menon* didn't know what to look forward to in the future. And it was amidst this ambiguity that his phone rang again. This time it was from a number from Delhi. *Menon* smiled because *Rashi* had been calling him from this number whenever she could to update him on the progress of various events in Delhi.

"Jai Hind sir, it's me, *Rashi*, we did it sir". And then she went about narrating the entire sequence of events including the ordeal at the drill square. "Why didn't you tell me all these when you were speaking to me almost every second day?". The answer given by *Rashi* would make a significant impact on the way *Menon* undertook the future mission in his life. "Sir, I didn't want even a single negative thought in you regarding my performance. I knew that if I had told you about my medical condition, you would discourage me from participating and for my well-being you would have told me to pull out of the competition and get medical help. Since I didn't tell you, you kept encouraging me to perform well and I didn't want to lose out on that. I had too much at stake". She paused possibly to overcome her emotions. *Menon,* couldn't control his. The immense joy of being able to ingrain in his cadets the philosophies for successful living flowed down his cheeks. He was thankful that the seats next to him were vacant and he could experience the bliss unhindered and unrestrained. *Rashi* continued "Sir, you told us that we attract realities based on our vibrations, I knew the faith that you had in me. I didn't want your vibrations on my performance to change. I didn't want your thoughts to change. You were my source of courage and strength to overcome the odds. I could withstand the physical pain but I would not have been able to withstand the withering of your belief in my ability to perform". *Rashi* stopped. There was a long pause from both sides. *Rashi* after having released her pent-up emotions of all these days which she had been unable to share with anyone else as no one else would have understood what she had to say, was now enjoying the tranquillity of release of her suppressed emotions. On the other side, *Menon* was being weighed down by the enormous weight of the realisation of the impact that his words had on these young minds. Thought waves were wandering at a quick pace between the past, present and future, one stimulating the other. He was thinking of the words of encouragement or otherwise that he had said to his cadets in the past and connecting them to the impact that had been made on *Rashi* and how the belief that *Rashi* had in him helped her to carve out her path to success. If the words that a mentor spoke held such significance for the cadet's success, then the words spoken to cadets with a negative connotation also must be having a crushing impact on the hope and morale of the cadet. Images of all the cadets who had been left behind in the race for selection to the directorate team flashed in front of him. His thoughts were also sprinting towards the future scenario and the role he must adorn to make maximum impact on the lives of others by making them realise their potential. After a considerably long silence, *Rashi* continued with the account of the events at Delhi. *Menon* enquired about others and was told about the performance of *Tarun* and *Mahesh*. He was overjoyed to know that the girl's team for the obstacle course, which *Saraswati* was also part of, had won the second position and each cadet was awarded the silver medal. *Menon* hoped that this achievement would take *Saraswathi* on an upward spiral of goal-setting and achievement. After

Rashi kept the phone, *Menon* drifted off to thoughts of the struggle and pain of the past, the joyful bliss of the present and the hopeful challenges that he would craft for himself in the future.

The train took a jerk, possibly due to it decelerating for an approaching station, or so he thought but it took *Menon* out of his reverie. He found himself being nudged by the Training Colonel "Dozed off eh?", the time for the written exam is over, we got to collect the answer sheets". *Menon,* got up slowly becoming aware of his surroundings and the reality that he was in the examination hall where the cadets for the Best Cadet event for Republic Day Camp were giving their written test for service subjects. This was the challenge that he had been visualising for the past few minutes while reliving the memories of the TSC competitions.

"Sir Flight Cadet *Shreya Sajeev,* Sir, Naval Cadet *Sahana,* Sir, Cadet *Sneha,* Sir, Cadet *Alwyn, Flight Cadet Gaffney, Flight Cadet Reshma*......the cadets were giving out their names as they deposited their papers at the invigilator's table. Each one was surprised at the big smile that one of the invigilators had on his face as if he had just won a lottery for a huge sum. For Menon, it was the start of a fresh journey of struggles, pain, challenges and the accompanying discovery of potentials and breaking of limits. The journey through the memory lanes had charged him with enthusiasm, hope and more importantly optimism. He was looking forward to the challenge that he had set for himself. The never-before-achieved challenge of winning all *The Nine Batons* by cadets of one single directorate.

www.ingramcontent.com/pod-product-compliance
Lightning Source LLC
LaVergne TN
LVHW091509170726
843492LV00001B/404